Psychic Development

for
Prosperity, Self-Defense & Political Influence

2nd Edition

Psychic Development

for
Prosperity, Self-Defense & Political Influence

2nd Edition

Kerth Barker

Psychic Development
for Prosperity, Self-Defense & Political Influence
2nd Edition

© Copyright November 1st, 2017 by Kerth Barker

www.psychicThreshhold.com

Acknowledgements

I would like to thank my friends Patricia Robinett and Richard Winkel whose continual help and encouragement made this book, and all my books, possible. I would also like to acknowledge the anonymous psychic, known to me as Deborah, whose extensive dialogues with me shaped the content of this final revised edition.

Book design by Author Support Coop

Disclaimer

This book is for educational and informational uses only and does not give advice regarding mental health treatment or medical treatment. Although this book may comment about the relationship between psychic training and mental health issues, this book does not give advice on mental health treatment and is not a substitute for mental health treatment when such is needed. The reader is solely responsible for any personal actions regarding mental health issues. Although this book may comment about the relationship between psychic training and physical health, this book does not give advice on medical treatment and is not a substitute for medical treatment when such is needed. The reader is solely responsible for any personal actions regarding medical treatment. This book is not advising the reader in the treatment of others concerning their mental health or medical condition. The reader is solely responsible for his or her actions regarding any such treatment of others.

INTRODUCTION

Developing psychic ability can be transformational. There are many stories I could relate to you. The first one that comes to mind is of a woman known to me as Deborah. It's not her real name, because of her need to remain anonymous, this was the only name she gave me. It was given to her by her psychic colleagues. They named her after a prophetess in the Bible.

Her psychic powers are amazing.

However, before she developed her psychic abilities, her life was rather sad. At a young age she clearly demonstrated a high level of intelligence. But when she became a teenager, she started to talk to her school teachers of having dreams that came true. At first they thought that she was just a bit eccentric. Then she began to have clear intuitive insights in which she knew the secret thoughts of her fellow students, as well as those of her teachers. This offended people, so one of her teachers labeled her as mentally ill.

The psychiatrists that she was turned over to were abusive. Deborah is a black woman. Some of the psychiatrists, who had authority over her in her youth, were white racists. They belittled and drugged her. This psychiatric abuse went on for years. Her struggles with them, along with the fact of being socially mislabeled as mentally ill, eventually drove her into homelessness.

Then one day she met a Christian psychic named James. He convinced her that she wasn't mentally ill, that she was instead profoundly psychic. She began training with him and other psychic Christians. She got off of the psych-drugs and off of the streets. She put her life back together. She eventually became a psychic consultant to a group of wealthy business persons. Now she is prosperous, lives in a nice home and is part of a secluded community of psychic practitioners.

She told me that she feels like she escaped hell and has entered Heaven. That's what psychic training did for her. So she was happy to help me create the final revised edition of this handbook for developing psychic abilities.

psyche: The mind and spirit.

psychic: An ability (or a person) that utilizes mental focus and spiritual awareness to acquire information or to influence change in the world.

gifts of the spirit: From 1 Corinthians 12 of the Holy Bible, this refers to spiritual gifts, given to believers, by the Holy Spirit; gifts such as wisdom, knowledge, healing, the ability to inspire others and the power to perform miracles.

psychic practitioner: Someone who has developed his or her psychic powers and uses them on a regular basis.

psychic threshold: This is the barrier that prevents you from accepting and using your natural inborn psychic abilities. The psychic threshold is something you must pass through in order to become a psychic practitioner. Passing through this threshold is the point in psychic training where the student is able to awaken psychic abilities so that they remain persistently present and useful.

The three major influences upon this book are *remote viewing*, *Christianity* and *Reiki healing*:

Remote viewing (RV) is a structured system of psychic perception developed by the U.S. government during the Cold War. For a period of years, I was in communication with some Christians who practiced remote viewing during the Cold War as well as some who were trained in remote viewing after the government ended its RV program. These Christians who studied remote viewing came to realize that they could make use of some of the techniques and concepts found in remote viewing to develop a new system for psychic development. With continual experimentation, this system evolved over time, and this book is the final outcome of that process.

This book doesn't teach remote viewing. RV is a highly effective system for an expanded perception of reality. But it is also a highly technical system that can take many months to master.

The system of psychic development, described in this book, is much easier and faster than RV. But you should know that certain remote viewing principles did inform the system of psychic development that this book explains.

This book is not a book on occultism, mysticism or New Age philosophy.

Christianity – This is a system that was originally designed by Christians for Christians. However, this system of psychic training has evolved over the years, so you don't have to be a member of a Christian church to learn from this system as it now exists. But you do have to at least be open to certain principles of Christian spirituality. This is not a book that teaches you the practice of the religion of Christianity. What it does teach is how to open yourself to the Holy Spirit, which is the active and invisible force that comes from our Creator. This connection with the Holy Spirit can help you in achieving your goals in life.

In the Bible, there are a number of passages which refer to miraculous healing taking place through a laying on of hands. For example, in Acts 28:8 the apostle Paul heals a man named Publius by praying and laying his hands on him.

Reiki healing is a system of healing developed in Japan which also heals through a laying on of hands. Not all Reiki healers are Christians, but some are. The word "Reiki" is a Japanese word that is often translated as "universal life force", but it can be translated in other ways. English speaking persons usually pronounce Reiki as "ray-key" but Japanese speaking persons usually pronounced it somewhat differently. It is made up of two words, "rei" and "ki". I don't speak Japanese, but a Japanese speaking Christian once told me that the word "rei" can be translated as Holy, and that the word "ki" can be translated as Spirit. So the word Reiki could be translated as Holy Spirit. And this is how the Christian Reiki healers who influenced this book translated the word Reiki. So for them, Reiki healing is really Holy Spirit healing.

If I'm not a Christian, why would I want to study this book?

Even if you're not a Christian, you may find that this system of psychic development is useful to you; nevertheless, as author of this book, I do understand why some people don't care for Christianity. If you are such a person, you may have had bad experiences with certain Christians. Although I am a Christian, I do know that some Christians can be overbearing or judgmental. You may have disagreements with Christians who are homophobic. You may have been raised in a Christian family that was dysfunctional. You may have been a member of a Christian Church that rejected you or with which you disagreed. You may see conservative Christianity as a political movement to which you are opposed. You may believe in a religion or philosophy other than Christianity. Or you may personally reject all organized philosophy and simply choose to believe in your own individualized view of things.

What you have to understand is that this is not a book on religion; it is a book that teaches psychic ability as a spiritual practice.

Consider this:
You can study yoga without being a Hindu. You can study mindfulness without being a Buddhist. You can study Tai Chi without being a Taoist. And therefore you can learn to develop your gifts of the spirit without being a religious Christian.

However, in the study of yoga you would use some Hindu

terms and concepts. In this spiritual system, described in this book, you will find some Christian terms and aspects of Christian spirituality. But you don't have to identify yourself as a religious Christian in order to use this system.

Isn't any Psychic practice a part of the New Age Movement?

The system of psychic development described in this book is different than that found in Wiccan practice, occultism, mysticism or New Age channelling. There are no practices in this book that actually conflict with traditional Christian theology. You won't be asked to worship false gods or graven images. You won't be encouraged to channel strange spiritual entities.

Are the practices in this book acceptable for all Christians?

Most Christians would have no problems with this system. Everything in this book is in agreement with basic Christian beliefs and the teachings of Jesus as found in the Bible. But the specific belief systems of Christian churches do differ. And some Christians do interpret the Bible in narrow-minded and dogmatic ways. So in all honesty, some persons who identify themselves as Christians might not find this book acceptable.

How does this system work?

There is a Creator who is the wellspring of all existence. From this Creator comes the active will and invisible force we call the Holy Spirit. Without the Holy Spirit, your human abilities are sadly limited, but when you attune yourself to the Holy Spirit, your abilities are greatly expanded. And when you are fully opened to the Holy Spirit, miracles become possible. And that's what it means to develop your gifts of the spirit, which are your divinely endowed psychic abilities.

But the Holy Spirit need not be thought of in religious terms. Reiki energy can be described as the universal life force.

Consider this:
The laws of nature are universal. The law of gravity applies everywhere on Earth and in outer space, and this is true of all time periods: past, present and future. The universal application of the laws of nature implies a single source of creation for all of nature. When your mind and consciousness is out of harmony with this source of all creation, you are disempowered because the universal life force ceases to be available to you. But you become empowered by regaining a harmony with this source of all creation because you then become opened to this universal life force.

So this system of psychic training consist of three aspects, all of which are intended to assist you in opening to the universal life force and developing psychic power.

These three aspects are:

1) Teachings about the functions of the psychic mind.

2) Teachings intended to assist you with making an attitude adjustment, conducive to psychic ability.

Such teachings consist of statements designed to confront wrong minded ideas, common to contemporary society, which place you intellectually out of harmony with the universal life force.

The validity of any teaching in this book may be questioned by you. Nobody expects you to mindlessly accept everything you read here, but in reading certain teachings, your thinking will be challenged.

So the purpose of some of the writings in this book are to get you to question some of your ingrained attitudes so that you can form a new way of thinking that allows for psychic ability. You don't have to agree with everything you read in this book, but you are going to have to learn to think outside of the box.

3) Training practices that you perform on a regular basis which will assist you in developing psychic powers.

Some of these training practices remove mental blocks to psychic power and some of them exercise mental abilities necessary to psychic power.

So this system of psychic ability consists of reading the lessons, in a sequential fashion, and performing the training practices on a regular basis.

The study of lessons and the training practices are structured to lead you up to a point where you work your way through the psychic threshold. There actually may be a number of psychic thresholds which you past through.

Once your psychic abilities emerge, how you access them and utilize them will depend upon your individual talents. And at some point you may find that you don't need the structure of training anymore.

How difficult is it to develop psychic abilities?

This really depends upon the individual. Everyone has differing potentials for psychic power and differing forms of latent psychic ability.

Everyone has latent psychic powers which are unused. Undoubtably this is true for you as well. You were born with psychic powers. But you were raised in a culture that taught you to suppress your natural psychic abilities. By the time you were an adult, you probably had completely lost touch with some or all of these natural psychic abilities. This has become the norm in our society.

So this is really a matter of reclaiming powers that have always been within you. The challenge that you'll face is in overcoming some of your social conditioning. This may or may not be difficult for you.

Some people put in very little work in developing their psychic powers, and yet in doing so they achieve a useful level of psychic ability. For many people, all they want to do is to enhance their intuitive abilities to such a degree that it helps them to achieve their goals in life. These are usually things like health, prosperity, romantic love, family, safety and happiness.

You probably had some goal in mind when you acquired this book. Perhaps you were just interested in seeing what it would be like to develop your psychic powers.

This book describes a course in psychic training. Every lesson exposes you to certain concepts that help in developing your psychic powers. Within each of these lessons you are given a description of a practical training drill. Some of these training drills are intended to be done only once, and some are intended to be repeated on a regular basis until your psychic abilities more fully emerge.

Other people have done this course before you, and in all honesty, not everyone makes it through all of these lessons. But most people do experience some degree of psychic awakening even if they only make it part way through the course.

But just reading the book will not awaken your psychic powers. You have to do the training drills if you expect to develop psychic ability. And this does require some effort.

I have known some students of this course who have developed profound and transformational levels of psychic ability. But this usually did require consistent work and dedication. The fastest time that anyone has successfully completed all of these lessons was about forty days. And usually it takes longer.

But there are some students that have spent only a week or so in study, never making it through all of the lessons, and yet have developed a useful degree of psychic awakening.

You are really the one who is in control. How far you go and the level of psychic power you attain is up to you.

How do I begin my psychic training?

I would be best if you studied this system with another open-minded and good-hearted person. It's ideal if you have a study partner; so your first step might be to find someone else to study with.

But if you choose to study alone, you can start your training right away. The lessons in the earlier sections of this book can be done by one person working alone. Eventually you will come across some lessons that do require a study partner if you are to do the training drills. Yet you don't have to do these later training drills in order to get the benefits from this system of training. So even studying by yourself, you can develop some level of psychic ability.

There are thirty lessons in this book, and some extra material in the Appendix. Even if you don't make it through all of the lessons, you may awaken some helpful degree of psychic awareness. You may find that you get what you want from this book even if you only make it through the beginning lessons. You'll have to decide how far you'll go. This book is designed to be studied in a sequential fashion. You'll get better results if you don't jump around by skipping lessons and trying to do the later ones out of sequence. So start with the first lesson.

. LESSON ONE .

When I was a young man in public school, one day I had an experience that changed my perspective on education. I had taken a test in history and one of the answers had been marked wrong.

The test question had asked, "Who first discovered the Americas?"

While taking the test I had been tempted to say that the Indians had discovered the Americas first, but the answer I actually wrote down had been, "The Vikings."

After she had marked that answer as wrong, I confronted the teacher. I pointed out that archeologists had discovered the remains of Viking settlements in North America which predated Columbus. The teacher replied that our textbook said that Columbus had discovered the Americas, and that we were being tested on the textbook, not on what we've learned in life.

After that I decided that I would never allow my education to get in the way of my learning.

Study as a form of meditation

Consider this:
The word telepathy is defined as mind to mind communication. Normally this is conceived of as talking without speaking. That is, one person would mentally speak into the mind of another person, although nothing would be said out loud. Some people call this "thought transference". Lesson Twenty-Two of this book explains a technique for authentic telepathy. If you work at this, over time, this is an ability that you and your study partner can achieve. But it's preferable if you don't jump ahead to this later lesson, because unless you do all of the preceding lessons, the techniques of Lesson Twenty-Two might not work for you.

Yet, in a sense, you can achieve another form of thought transference right away because you might also consider that the act of reading a book is a type of mind to mind communication. Without anyone speaking out loud, the reader is mentally receiving the thoughts of the author. So the process of studying a book is a form of receptive thought transference where information known to the author is transferred to the mind of the reader.

Many people have come to think of study as a tiresome chore. Certainly it is taught that way in schools today. But nobody here is going to expect you to memorize long lists of boring facts and you won't be tested or quizzed.

Instead, assume a serene attitude as you read. Study at a time and in a place appropriate for any other form of meditation that you might perform. Study for periods of forty-five minutes or less, and take breaks as needed to maintain your serene concentration. Psychic powers are best developed at a slow but consistent pace. It's best to study on a regular basis and have some daily practices; don't try to grasp this all at once.

Pay attention to what you feel as you study. Written words are the carrier waves in the mind to mind communication that takes place when you read. Written words, once read, can evoke an emotional response. They can guide behaviors. They can lead to understandings. They can impart useful knowledge. They can awaken abilities. This is the power of words.

There is a body-mind connection that takes place as you read. You may have already noticed this physical phenomenon: if you read a text that contains numerous words which you don't understand, you may begin to yawn and feel physically uncomfortable. You may even nod off or feel doped up.

When you feel this happening, don't drink caffeine and force yourself to go on studying. This is what students often do when they cram for a test. But cramming doesn't lead to real understanding.

Instead, try this. When you come across a word that you don't understand, look it up in a dictionary. Fully define the word. Make up some sentences with it. Then continue studying with a calm and lucid mind.

When you pay attention to what you feel in your physical body as you study, you can *actually feel* it when you've gone past words that you don't understand. So embrace your mind-body connection as you read. Be sensitive to your physical sensations of comfort or discomfort.

You're going to find that paying attention to your mind-body connection is important to your psychic development, so begin this practice with how you study. If you were taught speed reading in school, forget about that practice. What you want now is a deeper, more meditative, approach to reading. You want to feel your way through a text.

Study has an active component to it. Looking up words in a dictionary is an active process. Make a game out of this. Don't be irritated when you come across a sentence which contains a word that you've yet to apprehend. Look forward to finding a word that you don't fully understand. With a dictionary or other study tools, learn the origins of that *unapprehended* word and its different definitions. Find the definitions that make sense out what you are reading. Then fully define that word until you are lucid in its understanding. Have fun using your imagination to make up new sentences with the unapprehended word until you fully apprehend it.

If you have a good quality dictionary, it can be a useful tool in this meditation process.

The Journey is the Destination

In school you were probably told that the most clever of students are those who complete the lessons the fastest and who are best at memorizing the teachings in the lessons. But here, none of that matters. You are not in school, you are on a journey. This is a journey to develop your psychic powers. These are your gifts of the spirit. And this is a journey that will never end. So by beginning this journey, you have arrived at the destination you have sought.

This book describes a series of lessons. These lessons are a roadmap that will start you on your journey. Once you have completed the lessons you won't need a roadmap anymore. In the process of traveling through the lessons, you will eventually become a psychic practitioner. You will pass through psychic thresholds. You will learn how to use and develop your psychic powers on your own, without the need of any book. So as you work your way through the lessons, take your time. Enjoy the journey. Know that you have already arrived where you need to be.

Contained in every lesson are descriptions of training practices. Some of these are to be performed only once. Some are to be performed on a regular basis while your are training yourself to develop your psychic powers. Some might evolve into practices that you will use periodically for the rest of your life.

More than the lessons themselves, the use of these training practices will be what causes your psychic abilities to emerge. As you move through the lessons, you will probably spend an increasing amount of time performing the training practices. This is as it should be. The lessons serve a necessary purpose, but your performance of the training practices is what will cause your psychic powers to emerge.

If you were to read this book without performing the training practices, you might find it to be of some interest, but you would lose the opportunity to develop the extraordinary powers that sleep within you now, silently waiting for you to awaken them.

Training Practice

Recall one or more times that you read something and then applied what you read to accomplishing something in the world. In other words, recall a time when reading something gave you a new ability.

For example, perhaps you read a recipe in a cookbook and used it to prepare a meal that you and others ate. Perhaps you read some instructions that came with something you bought, and you used the instructions to build something or make a product operate in the way it was supposed to. Perhaps you used a driver's manual to help you operate a vehicle. Perhaps you took a course that had a textbook which explained how you could actually do something.

Think about this, and write down as many examples of this that you can recall. Write down specific examples, not generalized ones. If you have a study partner, share what you have written with him or her.

. LESSON TWO .

During the process of doing the final revisions for this book, I met with Deborah on a regular basis for a time. Because Deborah took her anonymity seriously, these meeting had a clandestine quality to them. We would typically meet on little-used side roads where we could sit in the back of her van and talk.

There was a protocol for these meetings. She would pick the date and time, but I would choose the exact location. There were numerous secluded side roads near the country home where I lived at that time. So there were many different locations from which I could choose.

The way that I would communicate the chosen location was that the night before the meeting, I would sit in a chair, close my eyes and visualize the place where we were to meet the next day. I wouldn't write the down location or say it out loud. The process of visualization was to only take place in my mind because Deborah would read my mind and that's how she knew the location. That was the only way she wanted it to be communicated to her. I never talked with anyone else about these visualized locations. The next day I would go to the location that I had visualized the night before, and her driver and her would be parked there already.

For a time I was tempted to believe that she wasn't really reading my mind, that she had hidden a GPS device on my car, that they were tracking it when I left the house, anticipating where I was headed, and showing up there ahead of me.

But one day I left for the meeting just as it was beginning to snow. The snow came down heavily as I drove. When I arrived at the meeting place, there was snow on top of the van and all around it. When I got into the van, Deborah smiled wryly, but said nothing about my doubts concerning whether or not she could read my mind. After our meeting I left the van to get back into my own car. As the van drove off, I noticed that beneath where it had been parked there was no snow at all. They must have been parked at that spot even before I left to meet them.

Psychic Culture

I have to tell you that the study of this Lesson Two may be difficult for some persons, and this may be because of emotional barriers. Some students might find this lesson an easy one to master, while others may feel highly challenged. And this has nothing to do with an intellectual understanding of what you read. If they apply themselves, anyone of normal intelligence can easily grasp what's being said here. But there is an issue of cultural shock.

There are two cultures on planet Earth right now. There is the larger, mainstream, culture of persons who don't use their psychic abilities. But also there is the smaller, secluded, culture of persons who do use their psychic abilities. The odds are that you, the reader, have grown up in the mainstream culture of people who don't use their psychic abilities. This

Lesson Two may be your first gateway into this secluded culture of psychics.

Some persons, even very intelligent persons, may feel some resistance to this process of cultural adaptation. I'm not saying that you are going to necessarily socialize with other psychics, but psychic awareness is a different way of thinking about the world. It requires a new attitude. And you may or may not feel comfortable in adopting this new attitude. I mention this now because it might be something you have to work through.

The basic theory of psychic ability is simple. Think of your entire body as being like an antenna designed to receive and transmit psychic energy. You first develop your psychic abilities by attuning yourself to the Holy Spirit, which could also be called universal life force or "Divine Source Energy". Once you've attuned to the Divine Source Energy, you do exercises that increase your mind-body connection. As you become hypersensitive to your mind-body connection, your psychic powers naturally emerge.

Divine Source Energy: This is the Holy Spirit, which is the invisible force and divine will that emanates from the Divine Source of all things. This Divine Source is the maker of all things both seen and unseen. If you've ever been involved with any Reiki healing or similar energy healing, Divine Source Energy is the universal life force that you direct while doing the healing.

Divine Source: This is God the Creator who is the source of all existence, visible and invisible, everywhere in the material universe and on the Spiritual Realm. Or you might think of this as an intelligent subatomic energy field that permeates the entire universe and out of which all material forms and electromagnetic energies are manifest.

Spiritual Realm: This is what some would call Heaven. It is a higher spiritual dimension of existence. It is a realm of pure love. The material universe is the world that we can see, hear, touch, smell and taste. We observe the material universe with our sensory perceptions. We observe the Spiritual Realm with our feelings of faith and our extrasensory perceptions, our ESP. The Spiritual Realm interacts with the material universe, but also transcends it. The Spiritual Realm isn't really separate from the material universe, although it may seem so. But the Spiritual Realm is not an abstract idea. With training you can come to sense the reality of the Spiritual Realm in your everyday life.

The terms *Divine Source Energy, Divine Source* and *Spiritual Realm* are terms that have been taught to me by an anonymous Christian psychic known to her students as Deborah. She feels it's best that persons training to become psychic be given a new terminology. A new terminology allows you to think of these concepts in a new way. These three concepts have been around for thousands of years, but if you think about them in a new way, you can more easily develop your psychic powers, which are your gifts of the spirit.

In this lesson we are going to explain psychic ability in an intellectual way. But actually it's best if you understand psychic ability in an intuitive way. Nevertheless, we start off with the intellectual explanation of psychic ability so that you can transcend it.

As you go through the following lessons, you will learn to feel how psychic ability works; that is, you will learn to intuitively sense how psychic ability works. But it's important that you first satisfy the analytical part of your mind so that you can let go of any tendency to continually intellectualize the process. *An intellectual understanding of psychic ability will not give you psychic powers.* But it can give you a framework for thinking about psychic powers, and this frees you to trust your intuition.

As you do the training exercises in this book you will use your intuition and develop it. This structured development of your intuitive powers will cause your natural psychic abilities to emerge.

Non-locality is reality

A non-local connection is a connection to something which is not in your local area. When you call someone on a phone, you are making a non-local connection with that person.

However, the significance of non-locality to psychic phenomena has to do with the science of quantum physics. This science studies quantum particles which are a measure of subatomic forces. *Quantum non-locality* refers to the fact that quantum particles have been shown to sometimes have non-local connections with one another. They may be many miles apart from one another and yet the behavior of one quantum particle may be entangled with the behavior of another one. There appears to be no known cause and effect mechanism of the material universe which connects these particles together. That is to say that you can't explain this phenomenon with Newton's laws of mechanics.

This phenomenon of *non-locality* was known to the Stanford Research Institute's research scientists who worked on its psychic research program that took place during the Cold War. They sought to develop techniques that would allow a human mind to make a non-local connection with another human mind. They also developed techniques for a human observer to make non-local observations of places and events. This would come to be known as *remote viewing*.

Quantum physics is one of the most well established disciplines of science. Many of the most advanced scientists in the world recognize that, although it may seem counter intuitive, non-locality is a real phenomenon.

So for the purpose of psychic development the question is, how can you best take advantage of this universal quality of non-locality?

The answer to that question is found in neuroscience.

The Neuroscience of Psychic Ability

I am not teaching you a course on neuropsychology. But I do need to go into some information that the science of brain research has indicated.

The human brain has two hemispheres each of which, in a generalized way, can be associated with certain mental attributes:

left hemisphere brain traits: logic, reason, rationality, language, math, science and analysis. (Thinks with words or symbols.)

right hemisphere brain traits: emotion, imagination, intuition, spatial awareness, holism and visualization. (Thinks with emotional mental images.)

If I were trying to teach neuropsychology, I would explain this in a more complex way, but for our purposes here I'm going to put this as simply as I can. The conscious mind is associated with a dominance of the left hemisphere of the brain and the subconscious mind is associated with a dominance of the right hemisphere of the brain. But although they do represent two differing modes of thought, the conscious and subconscious minds do have a complementary relationship. And much of psychic ability has to do with the interplay between the conscious mind and the subconscious mind.

The subconscious mind and the conscious mind are separated by a barrier which is a partial absence of wiring between these two hemispheres of the brain. This allows the brain's functions to be specialized. This ability for specialization has survival value. In our daily lives, we all go back and forth between these two modes of thinking. For example, when you are reading a book on sports you are using your left hemisphere brain functions, but when you immerse yourself in the playing a sport you are using your right hemisphere brain functions. When you are reading the book on sports your conscious mind is analyzing what you read. But when you are actually playing the sport, you don't have time to analyze what you're doing; you have to act with intuitive and instinctual certainty. And your intuitions and instincts arise from your subconscious mind. In living your life you are always switching the mental gears in your brain, sometimes using the left hemisphere (conscious mind) and other times relying upon the right hemisphere (subconscious mind).

A name for this mental barrier between the conscious and subconscious minds is the *limen*. This come from a root word that means threshold. In psychology the word *threshold* refers to a limit beyond which a stimulus fails to cause a reaction. So what goes on in one hemisphere doesn't stimulate a reaction in the other hemisphere. The word subliminal is derived from the same root word as limen. So anything that is subliminal is something which speaks directly to the subconscious mind or which involves the subconscious mind.

This brings up the question as to why the psychic threshold exists. And the answer is that society conditions people to lose their psychic abilities. You were born psychic. You still had psychic powers when you were a small child. But then you were trained and conditioned to lose your psychic abilities as you grew up.

The psychological barrier of the psychic threshold is created by social conditioning. The normal interaction between the left and right hemispheres of your brain has been interrupted by the process of education and socialization within our materialistic society.

Our present day society is not friendly to people with actual psychic abilities. This is why most of the psychics I have known have been very discreet in how they reveal such abilities.

You could say that our present day materialistic culture conditions people to suffer from spiritual deprivation. Psychic training is a way to overcome this spiritual deprivation.

The male brain and the female brain are wired in slightly different ways. One difference is that women have more wiring between the left and right hemispheres than men do, and this means that the connection between the left and right hemispheres is more prominent in women than in men. So this is why women are generally more intuitive than men. Perhaps it would be more accurate to say that women can more easily integrate intuitive thinking with logical thinking. This integration of logic with intuition is essential in psychic ability, so women often find it easier to train themselves to become psychic.

However, with training a man can develop his intuitive abilities. Understanding how the brain works is essential to this. The female brain can more easily integrate left and right brain functions. The male brain is more inclined to move back and forth between two different conditions of left brain dominance and right brain dominance.

Men are more dualistic in their mental functions than are women. When men are logical, they are very logical. For example, young boys generally find it easier to learn math than do young girls. Yet there are times, however, when men seem devoid of logic and rely solely on instincts or emotional thinking. In activities like aggressive sports and hand-to-hand combat, this type of emergence into instinctive emotionality can have its advantages.

So one might say that nature has neurologically designed

men and women in slightly different ways to solve the problems of survival. The male brain and the female brain represent two different, but complementary, neurological strategies for survival.

What this means for men who wish to develop psychic abilities is that we must work slightly harder. A man training to become a psychic can compensate for the advantage that women have in developing intuitive skills; he can do this by being more disciplined and determined in his approach to psychic training.

At the back of the brain is the visual cortex. This is the part of the brain that receives and processes information from the optic nerves. But the visual cortex isn't just involved in processing optical information. Neurologists have observed that the visual cortex is still active in persons who have been blind for life. This is because this part of the brain is involved with conceptualizing the surrounding environment and what goes on there. Sighted persons use visual information to conceptualize their surrounding environment. However, blind persons use their other senses such as hearing; although, even without the faculty for vision, it is still the visual cortex which is involved in their conceptualization of the environment.

This suggests a deeper meaning as to how the visual cortex operates. The visual cortex is vital in understanding your personal relationship with your surrounding environment. Consider the fact that both of the brain's hemispheres use the visual cortex. The visual cortex connects the left and right hemispheres. The visual cortex is able to incorporate both modes of thinking. So it is like a doorway which connects two rooms together.

The left and right hemispheres communicate with one another through the activities of the visual cortex. Via the visual cortex, the subconscious mind sends messages to the conscious mind in the form of visions such as those which you experience in sleep dreams. Via the visual cortex, the conscious mind sends messages to the subconscious mind through daydreams and imagination. So it is important to be clear in understanding the nature of the conscious and subconscious minds.

As infants, all boys and girls are more dependent upon the right hemisphere for their thinking because they haven't yet learned language. As children grow up, they learn more language and become more dependent upon the left hemisphere for thinking. So the *consciousness* of the child slowly shifts from the right hemisphere to the left hemisphere which then becomes dominant in thought processes. So the adult mind is the *conscious* mind which depends more upon left hemisphere thinking than upon right hemisphere thinking. Thus the childlike mind that is involved with right brain thinking becomes the subconscious mind because it becomes subordinate to the adult conscious mind of rationality.

superconscious mind: This is the aspect of mind which transcends the ego and the physical body. In religious terms, it's the mind of the soul. It is your spiritual body.

Your spiritual body will survive the eventual death of your physical body. Your spiritual body fills and surrounds your physical body. It is the essential spiritual consciousness that resides in your physical body and it is the aura that surrounds your physical body.

This superconscious mind is essentially spiritual and it's the source of psychic abilities. The superconscious mind communicates with the Spiritual Realm. Your superconscious mind is the spiritual body that lives continually in the Spiritual Realm. So the superconscious mind is above and beyond the intellectual limitations of the conscious mind. And the superconscious mind transcends the powers of the subconscious mind.

But while you are physically alive in this incarnation, your superconscious mind can be in a sleep-like state. And this is the condition that most human beings are in right now. Through spiritual experiences, you awaken your superconscious mind. And when that happens, you become more fully aware of the Spiritual Realm.

An analogy that might be used is that the Spiritual Realm is like the internet and the superconscious mind is like a computer terminal which gives you access to the internet. The Divine Source is the wellspring of all knowledge and the Spiritual Realm is the home of the Divine Source, and as such it contains all knowledge. When your computer accesses the internet, it is accessing a source of greater information. When your superconscious mind accesses the Spiritual Realm, you are accessing a source of greater information.

The thought processes of the superconscious mind and the substance of the Spiritual Realm are difficult to explain in words. Again there is an analogy which might help.

A *holographic image* is a three dimensional picture made with laser light beams that reflect off of a *hologram* plate. Like a statue made of light, the holographic image looks different depending upon the angle at which you view it. And unlike a two dimensional photo, every part of a hologram contains all the information contained in the whole. If you were to cut photograph in half, you would lose half of its visual information. But if you cut a hologram in half and project a holographic image from it, such an image would still be whole, although it would be visually less resolute.

Holographic intelligence is based on the principle that all of the object is contained in every part. For example, all of the laws of nature are contained in every location of the material universe. This is why the laws of nature are universal.

So the Spiritual Realm and your superconscious mind are based on what might be described as *holographic intelligence* contained in spiritual forms. From any point in the Spiritual Realm you can feel the presence of the Divine Source. And everything that has taken place, is taking place and will take place in the material universe is known to the Divine Source. Your spiritual body (which is your superconscious mind) is connected to your living physical body. But your spiritual body lives eternally in the Spiritual Realm. When you fully attune your conscious mind to your superconscious mind, all knowledge becomes available to you.

If this seems illogical to you, don't worry. It's impossible for human logic to fully comprehend the superconscious mind because it transcends the logic-based conscious mind. However it is important to note that one aspect of the subconscious mind is that it's more holistic in its thinking than is the conscious mind. So this is one reason why the subconscious mind more easily relates to the superconscious mind. Both the subconscious mind and the superconscious mind think holistically, but the conscious mind thinks in a logical, sequential way. Concepts like holographic intelligence can only be partially understood with logic, you must grasp them intuitively in order to comprehend them. Logical analysis will only take you so far, intuition completes the journey of true understanding.

Some studies into psychic research indicate that children are naturally more psychic than adults and that their natural psychic abilities decrease as they become older. Because of their lack of language skills, young children have to be super-intuitive. So the subconscious mind, which developed in childhood, is the key to superconscious, psychic abilities.

The superconscious mind is the source of your psychic abilities. The subconscious mind is emotional, imaginative and intuitive. Its thinking is not based on words or numbers. Yet it is these qualities of intuition and imagination which make the subconscious mind receptive to the superconscious mind. The thinking of the conscious mind is based on language and logic, but the superconscious mind has knowledge that transcends the limits of human language and logic. Thereby, the subconscious mind better translates the transcendental knowledge of the superconscious mind. But any information that is contained in the subconscious mind, can through training, be translated in a useful way into the conscious mind. *The conscious mind can receive psychic information through the subconscious mind.* So communication between the subconscious mind and the conscious mind is the key to awakening psychic powers.

The visual cortex is one pathway between the conscious and subconscious modes of thinking, but there is another. The nervous system of the physical body also connects the two hemispheres.

More than anything else, what the conscious mind and the subconscious mind have in common is the physical body. The left hemisphere of the brain and the right hemisphere are divided by the limen, but they are connected to each other through the body's nervous system. So a sensitivity to feelings in the physical body allows for communication between the left hemisphere and the right hemisphere. Also physical actions use the body's nervous system to allow communication between the left and right hemispheres.

Thus the conscious mind and the subconscious mind do have a dialogue with one another through physical sensitivity and physical actions. Therefore physicality along with visual processes are two doorways between the conscious mind and the subconscious mind.

There is a Spiritual Realm which connects everything and everybody in the material universe. When you understand the true nature of the Spiritual Realm, you realize that it is essentially made up of pure spiritual love. And this is what Heaven is, a realm of pure spiritual love. And the environment of Heaven is made up of all of the expressions of love. There are expressions of love in the material world, but let's face it, there are also many loveless aspects to life in the material world. The only things in the material world that last forever are those things which are expressions of true love. All of the loveless aspects of the material world will pass away.

So an awakening of your awareness of spiritual love is essential to the awakening of your superconscious mind-powers. The superconscious mind allows you to interact with this Spiritual Realm. And it's the subconscious mind which most easily attunes itself to this superconscious source of psychic information. Your intuition or feelings of faith can help awaken you to the wisdom and power of the Divine Source who acts through the Divine Source Energy.

You develop your intuition by paying attention to what you feel in your physical body. When you want to receive psychic information, pay attention to what your body is feeling or allow your physical actions to be guided intuitively. When you want to transmit either psychic information or psychic energy, you use your imagination and you act out physically in some way. When you meditate you are quieting your mind and relaxing you physical body so that you can become deeply sensitive to it. This deep physical sensitivity allows you to feel the presence of the Divine Source Energy that is within you and this connects you to the wisdom of the Divine Source.

The further lessons in this course will teach you to train your mind and your body so that you remove the barriers that prevent you from accepting the wisdom that comes from the Divine Source. You will learn to better open yourself to Divine Source Energy. And you will learn to receive information from the Spiritual Realm. All of this will make it possible for you to live a better life in the world.

Training Practice

From now on, at the end of every lesson, check in with your mind and body connection. As you have made it to the end of this lesson, I want you to do something. I want you to pay attention to what you feel in your physical body.

- Have you been yawning?

- Do you feel any confusion?

- Does your understanding of this lesson feel lucid? I don't care if you think that you understand this lesson, do you feel the truth of this lesson inside yourself? Do you feel good right now?

If you have any feelings of doubt about this lesson, I challenge you to make the decision to restudy it, either now or later. Use your dictionary or other research tools in a liberal way. Restudy this Lesson Two (as well as Lesson One and the Introduction) until you feel that you have fully apprehended the significance of what you've read.

Remember this:
You are a child of the Divine Source. All of the knowledge of the universe has always been inside of you. When you learn something new, you are merely awakening to knowledge that is already there. The lessons in this book are not academic, they are practical. If you apply yourself to studying them, they will awaken an ability that sleeps inside of you now.

. Lesson Three .

If we could read the secret history of our enemies, we should find in each man's life sorrow and suffering to disarm all hostility.

Henry Wadsworth Longfellow

Psychic Protection

There can be a dark side to psychic ability. It's not that the source of psychic powers is in any way evil. The Divine Source is all good, all loving and all healing. But we were created with free will. And there are people and spiritual beings who choose to do harm rather than good. So if you are going to learn to develop your psychic powers, you need to first learn to protect yourself from those who would abuse their psychic abilities to attack you in some way.

I'm not going to get into some complex philosophical discussion about why the Divine Source allows evil to exist in the world. Put simply, on a cosmic scale, the world we live in is like a playground for school children. In this playground there are some bullies. The teachers let us play in the playground with the hope that we will learn to stand up to these bullies. Then the bullies will stop being bullies. So if you're going to enter the playground of psychic ability, you're going to have to learn to protect yourself from psychic bullies. And here's how you do it.

- First, assume a physical attitude which conveys a sense of reverence.

- Second, say a prayer or positive affirmation requesting spiritual protection.

- Third, visualize yourself receiving spiritual protection.

- Fourth, reinforce the prayer and visualization with a physical gesture.

In saying a prayer or positive affirmation you need to learn to bring in physicality and visualization into the practice in order to bring out your full spiritual powers. Many religious movements use a combination of physical movement and mental concentration in their rituals. If you look at traditional spiritual practices throughout the world, you find physical disciplines such as those in Yoga or Tai Chi. This sort of mind-body awareness is necessary no matter what your religious or non-religious philosophy.

Spirituality and Religion

If you are a religious person, you may wish to be discreet in revealing your interest in psychic ability to your church. Spiritual power is the best defense against psychic attacks. And, in some cases, religion can be a source of spiritual power. But you need to understand the difference between religion and spirituality. Religions often seek to control a person's beliefs and behaviors. But spirituality is the emotional experience of feeling your unity with the Divine Source. Whether you describe this experience as faith in God or as an intuitive awareness of the spiritual aspects of the cosmos, this is primarily an emotional experience rather than an intellectual one. You can be spiritual without being religious, or religious without being spiritual. A religion is useful to the extent that it encourages spirituality. But in some cases, religions suppress spirituality.

As a Christian, what I personally believe is that God is love, God is the Creator of all things and that God is good. Religions, on the other hand, can be good or bad. Although I am a Christian, I know that some Christian churches are very toxic. And non-Christian religions can be toxic as well. Sometimes religious experience can enhance psychic ability. However, sometimes religious dogma can limit psychic ability. For me, psychic abilities are my God given gifts of the spirit. But some dogmatic religious leaders would use fearful judgements to condemn all those who believe in psychic ability.

If you are a member of a Christian church that automatically condemns all psychic power, your fellow members may not be happy with the idea that you are trying to develop psychic ability. And their negative feedback could inhibit your psychic development.

Yet if you do have a connection to a religious group that is positive and life affirming, your positive emotional experiences with them can help to protect you from mean-spirited psychic attacks. But if that's the case, you don't have to necessarily share with your fellow church members your personal interest in psychic abilities.

I know a number of very powerful psychics, and all of them are very discreet about revealing their psychic powers. It's usually best to only talk about psychic ability with other psychics or with those who are trying to develop psychic powers. You're not doing anything wrong by developing psychic powers, but spiritual practice is a personal thing. You don't need to share with everyone about your experience with psychic development.

Many people have a negative reaction to psychics because of irrational fears. Love is the essence of true spirituality, but chronic fear suppresses spirituality. So whether you believe in a religion or a non-religious philosophy, you can only develop a positive spirituality by rejecting irrational fear and developing spiritual love.

No matter what your religious or non-religious philosophy, you have the potential to develop psychic ability.

Psychic Shielding, Training Practice

When you pray or use positive affirmation you are attuning yourself to the Divine Source Energy. Below is a set of positive affirmations (prayers) any of which can be used to evoke the spiritual protection of the Divine Energy Source.

I'm going to suggest a visualization. After saying the prayer or positive affirmation close your eyes and imagine that there is a beam of divine light coming down from above. Imagine that it enters into the crown of your head. It fills your entire body and then emanates out from your body. Not all persons find it easy to visualize things in their minds. So you can support your ability to visualize by quietly vocalizing or subvocalizing the visualization. That would mean that in a whispered voice you would describe the visualization so that your visual cortex will translate it into images that will be accepted by the subconscious mind.

Subvocalize this:
"I now see a beam of divine light come down from above. It flows like clear glowing water. It enters the crown of my head. I feel it in my heart center. It fills my entire body. It glows outward through my aura."

I'm going suggest that you now repeat the above statement over and over again for as many times as necessary until you have it memorized.

You also need to know how a simple awareness of physicality can be involved in prayer. The position or attitude of your body communicates to your subconscious mind. A traditional prayer position is to hold your hands together at the center of your chest at the heart level. Your head is bowed. You are either sitting or knelling. Your eyes are closed. When you assume this body attitude, notice how it mimics the body position of an embryo in the womb. The memory of being in the womb is contained in your physical body. Your physical body contains a memory of its prenatal experience; this was an experience of being unconditionally loved by your mother and being embraced completely. So by assuming the prayer position, you are physically communicating (with body language) the idea of an acceptance of unconditional love.

I'm going to suggest that you practice prayer or affirmation for protection in this way:

1. Assume the prayer position described above.

2. Speak out loud saying a prayer or positive affirmation.

3. Visualize a beam of divine light coming down and filling you.

4. Touch your heart center then your forehead to physically indicate that you want love to protect and guide your psychic powers.

The more often that you practice prayer, the more powerful it becomes. Eventually you will begin to feel yourself being filled and surrounded with loving spiritual energy. It is good to be alone (or only with your study partner) and in a quiet place when you practice this type of prayer. Such prayer opens you to an awareness of the Spiritual Realm and it evokes the spiritual protection of the Divine Source Energy. There are many different prayers that you can use.

The following prayer is one that I have used and I know of other Christian psychics who have used it. It was written by the minister James Dillet Freeman.

Prayer for Christ's Protection

The light of Christ directs me; the love of Christ enfolds me; the power of Christ protects me; the presence of Christ upholds me.

Later the author of that verse came up with an altered version of it which has become widely known and used. I have known of Christians and persons of other faiths who have used this prayer. So it is a universal, interfaith prayer for all who believe in God.

Prayer for Protection

The light of God surrounds me; the love of God enfolds me; the power of God protects me; the presence of God watches over me; wherever I am, God is!

I knew of some atheists who were interested in developing their psychic abilities. They asked me for a positive affirmation that they could say which made no reference to God. I came up with a variation to the Prayer for Protection. I believe that James Dillet Freeman would not be offended. After all, Christ demands that we love all people, and that would include atheists. No matter what your philosophy, the following affirmation is something that you can say to yourself to center yourself in spiritual awareness.

The Love Affirmation

The light of love surrounds me. The aura of love enfolds me. The power of love protects me. The presence of love watches over me. Wherever I am, love is, and all is well.

Before going on to the next lesson, practice this technique for evoking spiritual protection which is described in the steps 1, 2, 3, and 4 above.

Later lessons will teach you more about spiritual protection, but this is a good starting point. Practice this prayer today until you are comfortable with it. And while you are using this book to develop your psychic abilities say this prayer on a regular basis, perhaps at least once a day. Consistency and repetition are essential to the development of psychic ability. Today, after you finish reading this lesson, practice this four part psychic shielding technique over and over again until you feel you can do it automatically.

. LESSON FOUR .

Fantasy, abandoned by reason, produces impossible monsters; united with it, she is the mother of the arts and the origins of marvels.

Francisco Goya

How to Become a Psychic Athlete

The principles described earlier will only make sense to you as you start to use them. There are many types of training drills that you can do. *Just like in sports, the more you practice, the better you get.* In this drill here, described below, you are involving yourself physically in the act of receiving psychic information but you are also keeping your eyes open and paying attention to visual impressions. So you are actively linking your right and left hemispheres via your visual cortex and physical nervous system.

Your superconscious mind is your highest level of awareness. Your superconscious mind can access the Spiritual Realm. Much of psychic training involves techniques to make you more aware of your superconscious mind. Here is one of them.

Automatic Writing

There is a stream of consciousness drill that sometimes can awaken psychic ability in a person. I can't guarantee that you will get results from this drill the first time you do it. But for most people, this drill does awaken an awareness of intuition. And doing it will help to give you an idea about how psychic practice works, whether or not you have an immediate psychic response. The name for this practice is automatic writing.

Before doing this drill you should center yourself in a positive sense of spirituality. You might do this by saying a Prayer for Protection as described above in Lesson Three.

If you are religious you might also say a favorite religious prayer. If you are nonreligious you might say appropriate positive affirmations or meaningful quotes of philosophy. If you are a Christian you might want to have a Bible nearby. Whatever books or symbols help you to feel safe and spiritually centered should be on hand. If you practice meditation, perhaps you should meditate for a while first.

We don't want you to open yourself to any negative psychic sources; we want you to be in a state of mind where you are open only to a positive and loving source of spirituality. Don't mix drug use with psychic experimentation, only do this when you are sober. So only do this automatic writing drill at a time when you feel good, lucid and relaxed.

Automatic writing works like this

Sit at a table in a comfortable environment. This should be in an environment that is free of distractors such as bright colors, loud noises or anything that demands your attention. Make sure you are in a calm mood and have peace of mind when you perform this. If you feel angry or upset about something, don't do the drill until you have resolved your issue.

As you perform the drill keep your eyes open, but blink naturally as needed. Have a notebook in front of you. Concentrate on breathing slowly and deeply for a while until you feel alert and physically relaxed. Then say something like, "I open myself to the wisdom of the Divine Source."

After that, start writing or drawing anything that comes into your mind. Keep your hand moving continually. Write anything. Draw anything. If nothing immediately comes to mind, scribble on the page slowly and deliberately. You might write the same phrase or word over and over. Make up nonsense. Or just write down thoughts as they occur to you in your mind. Don't stop to correct spelling or grammar. Don't stop to appreciate what you've just written or drawn. Although you may blink in a natural way, keep your eyes open and look at what you are writing and drawing as you work. If you fill up the page, flip over to the next one. Just keep on going continually writing or drawing whatever comes into the stream of your consciousness. Don't stop or pause at all until you feel you are done. Do this for a few minutes.

Never say that you don't have the ability to create drawings.

Everyone has the ability to draw pictures. When you were a child you created drawings with crayons. In this automatic writing practice, you may find that creating drawings is preferable or that you should combine drawings with writing. These don't have to be artistic drawings. Childlike pictograms will do.

It's probable that you may have to do this drill more than once in order to get a meaningful result. If you play a sport like baseball, think about how much practice it took to get good at it. You probably didn't hit the baseball the first time you swung at it. This is also true for psychic training. It often takes practice.

But you might get some result the first time you try it. Some people who have trained themselves to do this automatic writing drill have found themselves receiving information from a higher source of spiritual wisdom. This can also be a way to connect with your inner spiritual wisdom. If nothing else, it will help you to develop your intuition.

When you are done with the drill, look carefully at what you have scribbled, drawn or written. Sometimes there might be words or symbols in the scribbles that you didn't consciously intend.

This training drill is really just an experiment. Different people get different results when they try this for the first time.

And you may have done this before. Even if you've experimented with automatic writing before, we'd like you to try this again in the context of this course.

Try doing this one time, either today, or sometime soon when you're in the mood.

You will be asked to do this drill again in a later lesson. If you don't get positive results from doing automatic writing today, it may be because there are things blocking your psychic abilities. In subsequent lessons you will learn how to unblock your psychic abilities. Then in a later lesson, you can try automatic writing again and see the difference in results after you've performed some drills designed to unblock your psychic abilities.

. LESSON FIVE .

A life lived in fear is a life half-lived.
Spanish Proverb

Fear or Love?

You best connect with your spiritual nature through your positive emotional experiences. Prosperity arises from love, not the love of money but rather the love of creativity. When your creativity and productivity reaps rewards, prosperity is the result. When approached with a creative and ethical attitude, the experience of prosperity can be spiritual. Loving sexual experiences can be spiritual as well. It's a loving attitude which leads to a life of spiritual experiences.

Such experiences are not the glee that might come with materialistic indulgence. A sex addict might feel gleeful when he indulges himself sexually in some perverse way, or a plutocrat might feel smugly superiority when he contemplates his wealth. These types of materialistic indulgences don't lead to a true emotional contentment and happiness. These fleeting feelings of glee which come from materialistic indulgences are based on either fear or on the baser animal instincts. The overly greedy plutocrat has a subconscious fear of poverty. The sex addict fears emotional intimacy.

Simple emotional intimacy with other people and with life itself is the essence of spirituality. When you hug a friend and feel that friendship physically in your body as love, that is a spiritual experience. When you enjoy being with a pet, that is a spiritual experience. If you feel joy in your heart when you are in a beautiful natural environment, that is a spiritual experience.

As a Christian, I have physically felt the feeling of fellowship throughout my entire body when I have prayed and worshipped with other Christians. I know that people of other faiths have had such experiences as well. I don't care what your personal philosophy is, spirituality is a human need. The development of a strong, positive spirituality is your best defense against psychic attack or manipulation.

When religion is based on a loving attitude it can be a source of positive spiritual experiences. But when religion is based on fear, it becomes oppressive and controlling.

I believe that there are many paths to the mountaintop, many paths to a positive spirituality. All of them favor love over fear. You must take into consideration the beliefs and practices which seem most natural for you and your peers. I try to understand as many different philosophical viewpoints as possible. This way I can relate to other people in explaining psychic ability.

The Psychic Matrix

I have known some psychic atheists who nonetheless believe that God exists, but they believe that God is an archetype which only exists within the psychic matrix of all human beings. So they reject a religious belief in God, but accept the concept of God as a phenomena of psychic power and psychology.

The word *archetype* comes from a Greek word that refers to something which is molded as a model. So, for example, a man who sells statues might make a model of a statue for his workers to imitate, and that model would the an archetype. In psychology and psychic technology, an archetype refers to something that represents data or presents data.

A *matrix* is a point or place where other things originate or develop. The root word for matrix is *mother*. A psychic matrix would be a group mind that arises from a subconscious psychic connection of people. A psychic archetype would be an entity or concept that is born out of the connecting field of psychic energy that forms a matrix.

So with that concept in mind, let me explain what my psychic atheist friends believe. They believe that all human beings are psychically connected on a subconscious level of mind through a *collective unconscious*. They see God as a *data system* within the collective unconsciousness of all human beings.

I believe that their theory is worth contemplating, even by those of us whose theology demands a faith in God. As a Christian, I believe that God is more than an archetypal data system. But I also think that this idea of *collective consciousness* does seem to have some merit.

The famous psychoanalyst Carl Jung believed that there was

a *collective unconscious* which connected all human beings together. You might conceive of this collective unconscious as ideas that are inborn into all people as instincts. However with an awareness of psychic abilities, you would also have to consider that the collective unconscious is a subconscious psychic connection, a field of psychic energy which forms a matrix that exists between all humans.

Within this collective unconscious lives archetypes. Jung defined these archetypes as symbolic representations of human beliefs. So according to this philosophy, God exists within this collective unconscious as an archetypal symbol. Thus, according to this philosophical viewpoint, when people pray to God in Church, they are evoking this archetypal symbol from the collective unconscious and experiencing it consciously.

Not all atheists believe in psychic ability, in fact many atheists deny that psychic ability could exist. These atheists who explained this theory to me, do, however, accept the existence of psychic abilities as a fact of science. Once you've witnessed or practiced remote viewing, it's hard to deny that psychic abilities exist.

So anyway, these atheistic remote viewers believe that God, Satan, demons and angels are all archetypal symbols within this psychic collective unconscious. They theorize that if everyone in the world were to stop believing in Satan and demons, the world would instantly turn into a living Heaven ruled by an archetypal God and served by archetypal angels. Personally I'm not an atheist, and I believe that God is more than an archetypal symbol, but I am amused by this theory.

And this theory makes a point about spirituality. I don't care how you intellectually justify a positive spirituality. It's more about emotions than about ideas. It's about developing love-based emotions and rejecting fear-based emotions. The essential conflict in humanity is between spiritual love and irrational fear.

I'm proud to be a Christian, but I do recognize that angry, judgmental Christians are lacking in a positive spirituality. Occult satanists deliberately evoke negative emotions and use them to project negative psychic energy toward others. This psychic projection of negative emotions is a satanic practice. Therefore a Christian who prays or preaches when he has anger in his heart is actually practicing satanism even if his theology is officially Christian.

Nevertheless, even an open-minded atheist with a loving attitude can have a positive spirituality. No matter what your theology, if you wish to develop your psychic abilities for healing purposes, you need to let go of irrational fears and concentrate on spiritual love.

Psychic Energy and Brain Structure

One way of understanding psychic energy is to look at the brain. At the base of the brain is a *reptilian brain*. This is a primal brain known as the *basal nuclei* because it is at the base of the brain and forms the foundational nucleus of the brain. This reptilian brain is surrounded by the limbic complex.

The word *limbic* comes from a root word that refers to the

edge of things, and the *limbic system* is on the edge of the lower reptilian brain as well as the higher brain. This limbic brain is found in other mammals and is associated with basic human feelings as well as basic physical drives.

The *neocortex* is the outer core of the brain which is associated with advanced human thought processes such as aesthetics, imagination, intuition, spirituality, intellect, language, math, logic and reason. Evolutionarily speaking, the neocortex is the new brain.

The reptilian brain is an older, survivalist brain. It thinks in terms of the *fight, flight or freeze* instinct. For example, when you feel threatened, you react with hatred, anger, fearful retreat or immobilizing terror. That's the reptilian brain hijacking your emotions and possibly your behavior. When the higher brain functions of the limbic system or the neocortex are inhibited, the lower reptilian brain can take over and drag your emotions and behavior down into negativity.

The highest level of psychic energy is associated with those mental activities that relate to the neocortex. There is a field of invisible psychic energy that surrounds your body. This is an energy system that interacts with and is related to the brain and nervous system. The mind is more than the brain. The mind is also mental, psychic energies that interact with the electrical and chemical processes of the brain and nervous system. These psychic energies can be thought of as vibrational energies.

The higher vibrational energies are associated with the higher brain, and the lower vibrational energies are associated with the lower, reptilian brain. The high vibrational psychic energies are the most powerful.

Occultism and Secret Societies

Satanic occultism is based upon evoking the lower vibrational psychic energies. The word *occult* means hidden. Often times people hide things because they are ashamed of them. In occult practices, deviant sex or violence may be used to evoke lower brain functions. The psychic energies created from these lower brain activities are of the lower, negative psychic vibrational energies. However, when these negative psychic energies are skillfully directed toward people who are naive about the existence of occultism, they can be used to successfully attack and manipulate them.

When higher vibrational (positive) psychic forces are evoked, they are more powerful than the lower vibrational (negative) psychic forces. So, for their occult powers to work, the satanic occultists need for the general population of humanity to be ignorant of psychic abilities. Most people are good, and would prefer to use their psychic powers for loving, positive purposes. The secret societies of occultists can only have power by keeping the general population in the dark concerning the truth of psychic power. So long as this small minority of occultists are using their psychic abilities and the majority of the Earth's population are ignorant of their psychic powers, this small group of occultists are very powerful. But as a general awakening of psychic awareness takes place in the world, these satanic occultists will be defeated.

Angels and Demons

If you start to develop psychic abilities, you will come across angels and demons. You may think of them in different ways, depending upon your philosophy.

You may think of them in terms of traditional religion, which is how I personally think of them. But I like to consider other points of view.

You may think of them as the phenomena of psychic energy and psychology; that is, you would think of angels and demons as archetypes in the collective unconscious of humanity.

You may also think of angels as the psychic presence of benevolent extraterrestrials. And in this way of thinking, demons would be conceived of as the psychic presence of hostile ETs. And there is a great deal of information suggesting that extraterrestrial intelligence does exist. So I don't automatically discount this theory.

But make sure of this one truth, angels and demons are in some sense real.

The focus of your emotional awareness determines how your psychic energy is projected. Therefore it is better to contemplate the loving Divine Source and the loving angels than to contemplate fearful symbols or ideas.

Angels are the servants of the Divine Source. They never evoke fear, they only evoke love. An angel will never encourage you to worship it. The angels only want you to worship the Divine Source. The angels know that God is love.

The angels will never try to possess you. But they will provide loving guidance if you ask for it. They are messengers of the Divine Source. Angels are the citizens of the Spiritual Realm. Angels will guide you to accepting Divine Source Energy.

Angels are invisible, but you can physically feel their presence as love. When an angel is present, you will have a positive physical sensation of some type, often at your heart center or at the crown of your head. Angels are not merely intellectual constructs, they are energetic beings, and their loving energy can be physically felt. Sometimes a pleasant floral smell may accompany the invisible presence of an angel.

Pictures and statues of angels should never be worshipped, no angel would want that. But such representations can be lovingly contemplated as a way to evoke the presence of angels. For example, when I evoke an angel to assist in defending me from an intentional satanic occult attack, I sometimes contemplate the image of the Archangel Michael. I have known other psychics who have successfully defended themselves from satanic occult attacks; some of them have put images of various angels around their homes. This has nothing to do with superstition. And it isn't based on fear. It's based on love. Representations of angels are symbols of love, healing, faith and courage.

However, in contrast, demons are deceptive and cruel. They hate humanity and desire to destroy us. Demons will try to turn you away from the worship of the Divine Source. They will deny the Spiritual Realm. They will invalidate your positive spirituality. They will use facts in a distorted manner to conceal the truth of things.

Demons are invisible, but you can feel their presence as intense feelings of terror or hostility. Their negative emotions can cause sickness in people. They enjoy creating mental confusion. They enjoy tricking people into doing degrading things. The smell of burning sulfur may accompany the presence of a demon.

Demons may promise you wealth or sexual indulgences if you do as they command. They seek to control you and to possess you. Their goal is to bring your soul under the possession of Satan who is the personification of all evil.

As I have tried to point out, you can understand the phenomena of God, Satan, angels and demons in different ways. You may think of these phenomena in terms of the psychic matrix which is the collective unconscious of humanity and the archetypal symbols contained within it. Perhaps demons are mental parasites that live within the negative thoughts of confused human beings. You may think of these phenomena in terms of traditional religion. You may put these phenomena into the framework of a belief in extraterrestrials.

Personally I find it easier to understand all of this through a simple faith in God who is loving and good. I don't feel the need to intellectually understand exactly what angels and demons are, I only need to understand my relationship with God. However, although I am a Christian, I try to understand the phenomena of angels and demons from as many points of view as I can so that I can relate to as many different people as possible.

But in a way, it doesn't matter how you intellectualize this. An encounter with and angel or a demon is an emotional experience. You will learn to recognize them by a sensitivity to your feelings. If you can tell the difference between the feeling of spiritual love and the feeling of unreasoning fear, you know the difference between an angel and a demon. The angels are empowered by your feelings of spiritual love, but the demons feed on your feelings of fear, anger and hate.

At some point in your psychic development, you have to choose sides in this ongoing battle between them.

The Matrix of Supernatural Fear

There is a type of psychic matrix of evil (a matrix of supernatural fear) that is presently being imposed upon humanity. I'm not trying to make you feel paranoid. In fact, I believe that the benevolent psychic power of the Spiritual Realm is greater than this evil psychic matrix. This evil psychic matrix may simply be the negativity that arises from the negative archetypes contained in the collective unconscious of humanity. This evil matrix may be the mind of Satan as described in the Bible. This matrix of evil may be a mental occult attack by hostile ETs. Whatever it is, it is real. It is as real as every unnecessary war that is now being fought. It is as real as the crushing poverty that is needlessly imposed upon so many people. It is as real as every starving child in the world. It is as real as every lie told by every lying politician. It is as real as every broken family and every drug addict on the streets.

There may be political and economic solutions to some of these issues, but in this textbook I'm going to mainly focus on this as a spiritual problem. You can't solve every problem that this world now faces, but you can disconnect your mind from the psychic force of this matrix of evil.

More importantly, you can better connect yourself to the love, peace and wisdom of the Spiritual Realm. You can attune yourself to the Divine Source. You can learn to accept and project Divine Source Energy. This is the essence of psychic self defense.

When you realize that this psychic matrix of evil does in fact exist, you can stop feeling resentment for those human beings who do evil. This is because you realize that those persons who are doing evil are themselves merely puppets of this evil matrix.

I personally believe that all human beings are born with the potential to be good. However, because of the nature of this world, we are all influenced, to varying degrees, into evil attitudes and behaviors. As the Bible metaphorically states, we have all eaten of the fruit of the Tree of the Knowledge of Good and Evil. So, there is for each of us the choice between good and evil as a lifestyle.

Some people allow themselves, of their own free will, to become the slaves of this evil occult matrix. And I believe that there are ultimate consequences for surrendering to this matrix of evil. Some satanic occultists deliberately accept this evil matrix because they believe that it will lead them to the fulfillment of lustful or greedy desires. But ultimately, those persons who knowingly accept this evil matrix into their consciousness suffer greatly.

So in realizing this, you can feel compassion for those human beings who have done evil, even while you renounce the evil that they have done. It is the matrix of evil acting through human beings which is causing all this harm, not the persons themselves. So this is a way for you to let go of resentment for any of your fellow human beings and to feel compassion for all of your fellow human beings.

Reverend Martin Luther King Jr. once said, "Love is not this sentimental something that we talk about. Love is creative, understanding good will for all men... When you rise to the level of love, of its great beauty and power, you seek to only defeat evil systems. Individuals who happen to be caught up in that system, you love, but you seek to defeat the system."

Psychic Self Defense and Mental Health

Furthermore, this evil psychic matrix doesn't just tempt some human beings to become corrupt, it is also a source of emotional oppression. I'm not going to try to diagnosis mental health problems for people I've never met. Nevertheless, I have known persons who have been told that they were suffering from depression, but the psychiatric drugs and the therapies didn't work. However, when they started to use techniques of psychic self defense, the depression and confusion stopped. Many mental health problems have been misdiagnosed. When you understand the true nature of the world, you realize that spiritual issues are at the heart of everything.

Avoiding Psychic Attack

There is spiritual warfare going on in this world at this time in human history. And whether you know it or not, you are under psychic attack. Everyone on this planet now is under a satanic occult attack. But once you learn a few simple principles and techniques, you can defend yourself and those you love.

Here are some common sense rules to help you avoid psychic attack:

- Don't dabble with occult practices or satanism. Many people who dabble with the occult or satanism find themselves being manipulated by dark forces. Don't experiment with such practices just to see if they work.

- Never use Ouija Boards. If you use an Ouija Board, you are inviting any type of spiritual being to come into your consciousness to manipulate you. This invites demonic possession or poltergeist visitation.

- Extreme use of drugs or alcohol can make you vulnerable to psychic attack or demonic possession.

- Never include skulls or bones, whether human or animal, on any altar at which you might pray.

Intentional and Unintentional Psychic Attack

It isn't just occult satanists who have practices for psychic attack. The intelligence community has experimented with psychic warfare for many years now.

Remote viewing research was conducted by US military intelligence after WWII during most of the Cold War. Remote Viewing is a highly structured form of extrasensory perception. Controlled remote viewing involves exact protocols and is based on numerous principles. It was conceptually developed by the Stanford Research Institute and used for many years by military intelligence in the USA.

Remote Influencing is a closely related psychic discipline. With Remote Influencing, the health, beliefs or behavior of a subject can be shaped by the remote influencer. First the subject is remote viewed, and then the remote viewer tampers with the subconscious mind of the subject. Remote Influencing can be used to heal someone, and it's ethical to do so if you have permission from the subject. But some psychics use Remote Influencing for unethical purposes.

If you think that some unethical person is trying to use Remote Influencing to harm you, one thing you can do is to start paying attention to your dreams. Dreams are the key to understanding your subconscious mind. And Remote Influencing is directed toward the subconscious mind. So by writing down your sleep dreams after you wake up, you are bringing your own will power and consciousness into the subconscious realm. This makes it harder for you to be manipulated against your will through the subconscious tampering involved in psychic attacks.

As well as deliberate attacks, you may be under psychic attack from an untrained person who is using his or her psychic abilities unintentionally. If you are in a relationship with a person who is controlling or hateful, that person may be directing intense levels of negative psychic energy toward you without really understanding what he or she is doing.

Ethics and Psychic Self Defense

So there is another principle that you should realize and that is that ethics are necessary to psychic self defense. If you attempt to use your psychic powers to manipulate other people against their will, you make yourself vulnerable to psychic attack.

I know that you have been told that we live in an amoral universe. You have been told that the universe is a giant unfeeling machine. Some have told you that there is no God and no afterlife. Therefore there is no higher spiritual authority which could judge the morality of your behavior.

And there are some modern philosophers who have said that morality is a weakness. This type of intellectual rejection of ethics has become common.

But in fact the Spiritual Realm operates on the basis of ethics. If you use your psychic powers in unethical ways, you weaken your ability to defend yourself psychically. For whatever reason, that's just the way it is. So if you are intentionally using your psychic powers, you have to use them in purely ethical ways. This means that if you want to maintain your highest level of psychic ability, you must only use your psychic abilities to heal people and to defend the innocent. The unethical use of psychic abilities weakens your psychic powers.

If the Divine Source is all good and the Spiritual Realm is all good, you may wonder: how could any evil exist?

You may not like the answer. You may think of yourself as an old and wise spiritual being, but we Earthlings all are just children in the spiritual playground of the universe. We have free will, and we can use our powers to be good children or naughty children. Someday we will be powerful spiritual beings who live forever in the Spiritual Realm. Someday all of the suffering of this world will pass away, and all that will be left will be the lessons we have learned and the love that we have created. We are allowed to make mistakes so that we can learn from them. And those who choose to do evil are making a mistake.

I think most of the readers of this book desire to heal themselves and to heal others. In learning to use your psychic abilities to heal other people, you must first learn to use them to heal your own life. You may heal yourself physically, emotionally and financially.

Most of the readers of this book desire to make an ethical use of psychic abilities. You may use your psychic powers to improve the political systems. You may use those insights which come from psychic practices to better your life. The angels might guide you to a better path to prosperity, for example.

But if you were to use psychic powers to steal from somebody else, that unethical use of psychic power would weaken your psychic shield and make you open to psychic attack. Both the Spiritual Realm of goodness and the matrix of evil have the ability to influence human beings. If you intentionally or unintentionally attune yourself to the matrix of evil, harm will come to you even if you do gain some worldly power. But if you intentionally attune yourself to the Spiritual Realm of goodness, you will heal your life as well as the lives of others.

A Loving Attitude is Your Shield

Your psychic shield is the energetic and spiritual aura that surrounds your physical body. It's not an abstraction; it's tangible. If someone were to photograph you with an infrared camera on a dark night, the heat which your body produces would be visible in the picture. But that thermal energy is only one aspect of your aura. There are other energies involved which cannot be directly measured with any type of device, but these psychic energies are nonetheless real. A strong psychic shield makes you less vulnerable to psychic attack. So anything that strengthens your psychic shield protects you.

One thing that can strengthen your psychic shield is an attitude of good will for all humanity and all living things. If you have a persistent attitude of good will for all people, and somebody tries to attack you through a psychic means, they will be influenced by your attitude. Before they attack you, they must psychically contact you. When they do this, your attitude of good will is likely to affect them, if only on a subconscious level of mind. But their psychic powers also have to be processed through their own subconscious minds. So when they try to remotely influence you, your loving aura will instead remotely influence them. This means that these psychic attackers are likely to change their minds and decide to not attack you. So the Biblical commandment given by Christ to love our enemies is actually very practical advice for psychics.

When people use their psychic powers, deliberately or unintentionally, for harm, they do so because they are caught up in an evil system of occultism. So you must reject the matrix of evil but feel compassion for the person who is caught up in it. The more you understand about the nature of satanic occultism, the more you can see this truth.

There is a culture of materialism, fear and anger which is being imposed upon humanity. It causes the individuals caught up in it to strike out in fear and anger. When they do so with their psychic powers, it can cause harm to you or those you love. Your greatest defense against these psychic attacks is the redemptive love of good will for all humanity. You can feel compassion even for those who feel hatred for you when you realize that they are being manipulated by demonic forces directed against humanity. I'm not saying that you should forget or minimize the harm done by those who have surrendered to this matrix of evil, I'm saying that it is to your practical advantage to have an attitude of forgiveness. I know that this is difficult. But this commitment to love for all humanity and all life is your greatest defense against psychic attack.

Divine Light Training Practice

You can reinforce your natural psychic shield with meditation and visualizations. One technique is to use visualization to imagine yourself surrounded by a bubble of divine light. But this should not just be a mental process. You should also involve yourself physically in this process.

- Remember that you consciously communicate to your subconscious mind with a combination of physical actions and imagination.

- When you close your eyes you invite imagination into your consciousness.

- The subconscious mind responds to these two things: first, the conscious thought of an imaginary mental picture, and then a physical reinforcement of that visualization which will energetically drive this expression of psychic power.

It's best to sit down in a comfortable chair when you do this meditation.

Meditate on the thought that your psychic shield is like a balloon and that every time you breath out, you are strengthening and expanding your psychic shield.

Before you practice this meditation, center yourself in serenity and love. Prepare yourself in whatever way seems appropriate. Say a prayer or a positive affirmation.

The light of love surrounds us. The aura of love enfolds us. The power of love protects us. The presence of love watches over us. Wherever we are, love is.

As you close your eyes and visualize, breathe slowly and deeply. As you breathe out, purse your lips as if you are blowing up a balloon, and visualize a bubble of divine light flowing into your aura and expanding out into the universe. You may subvocalize the words of the visualization in order to help make it real to you.

I see myself surrounded by a bubble of divine light. Every time I exhale, this bubble gets bigger and stronger as if I were blowing up a balloon. But this balloon of divine light will never pop.

Doing this visualization technique can unblock your psychic powers because it will release you from the negative psychic influences in the world.

You can do this visualization for five to ten minutes whenever you feel like it. The regular practice of this technique can reinforce your natural psychic shield. Also you can use this type of visualization to protect your loved ones. Imagine someone you care about surrounded by a bubble of divine light into which you blow love-based psychic energy. When you finish the meditation, open your eyes and breath normally for a while before you stand up. Please practice this technique now.

. Lesson Six .

I was told a story once by a woman who felt that she had been under psychic attack. She was attending a Christian church whose new minister was a man. When he first became leader of the congregation, he had asked her out on a date one day, and she said no. This happened a number of times, until he finally gave up. But he seemed to have a resentment toward her because of this rejection.

This woman eventually developed an interest in psychic abilities. She made the mistake of sharing this fact with another church member. When the minister heard of this, he reacted with anger. He started giving sermons on the evil of psychic abilities. He accused all psychics of being frauds or witches. The woman could feel the psychic anger coming from this man, and the negative judgement of the entire congregation fell upon her.

She left that church, but she continued to feel that the members of her former congregation, lead by this frustrated and angry minister, were psychically attacking her. So she decided to pray for the minister, asking God to eliminate his anger and frustration. Shortly after that, the minister fell in love with a different woman in the congregation and he calmed down and stopped preaching hatred.

The woman who told me this story eventually met up with some other Christians who did believe in psychic development and she was able to follow her desire to develop psychic abilities as a spiritual practice.

All People are Connected

I'm sharing this story with you because I feel that it's important to understand that having compassion for those who attack you is essential to psychic self defense.

Sometimes it's just common sense things which can strengthen your auric psychic shield. Taking care of your emotional and physical health helps you to have a strong aura. To favor healthy foods can actually influence your psychic abilities because how you treat your physical body does influence your psychic powers. Your aura is connected to your physical body. And physical-based spiritual practices such as martial arts training and aerobic exercise can be very helpful in strengthening your aura. Martial Arts training can also strengthen your psychic shield. Even if you aren't really good at Martial Arts, and even if you practice Martial Arts in a gentle or moderate way, it helps in developing a mental attitude which makes it difficult for you to be psychically manipulated. So understand that psychic ability isn't just a mental ability, it's a mind-body discipline.

Many people in our culture are encouraged to disconnect their consciousness from their feelings. When this attitude of emotional disconnection becomes too extreme, it's called disassociation. And disassociation is a form of mental illness. So being in touch with your feelings is essential. You must learn to pay attention to your emotions. When you are under psychic attack, you will usually feel physical sensations; it's common to have feelings of unease in your solar plexus and heart. If you do experience these sensations and feel that they might be the result of a psychic attack, it's a good idea to do something physical to process these negative feelings. Here are some things you can do to process negative feelings:

- Rhythmic drumming
- Chanting or singing
- Deep breathing exercises
- Doing an exercise routine
- Concentrating on a physical chore like gardening or cleaning house
- Taking a brisk walk

If you have a feeling that you can't escape a psychic attack, go someplace safe and start walking briskly or jogging. The physical movements will distance you emotionally from the psychic attacker.

What you should not do is be physically passive. Don't curl up in a fetal position and fall into a black well of depression. Don't sit in front of the TV eating junk food. Make yourself do something actively physical. You feel emotions with your body and you express feelings with your physical body. So understand that psychic self defense is a mind-body discipline.

Training Practice

Now for many people it is difficult to comprehend that

another person can psychically attack you from a distance or psychically heal you from a distance. So the following training exercise may help you to realize that you are psychically connected to other people.

This is another simple psychic drill you can do. I can't guarantee that this will work for you the first time you do it. However, it will help you to understand how psychic abilities can be used, and it will help to attune you to your intuition. In this drill you will read the mind of someone you care about.

First, create or find an environment that is conducive to doing a psychic reading. This would be a comfortable environment free of distractors. Remember that *distractors* are anything that might demand your attention. Some examples of these are food, hot or cold drinks, pets, people, bright colors, electronic devices, noisy machines, picture books and weapons.

Next, sit at a table with a pen and paper. Relax yourself and clear your mind. This is an eyes-open meditation because you don't want to invite imagination. You want the reading to be only of the other person's mind and not of your own fantasies about that person. *When you close your eyes you invite imagination.*

Before performing this meditation, say a prayer or a positive affirmation such as the Love Affirmation. On one piece of paper write down the name of a person for whom you only have positive feelings. Or you could use a photo of that person. Hold that name or photo in one hand. With your other hand, hold a pen or pencil.

Contemplate your intention for a few moments. It would be unethical to be a peeping Tom who might read something in a person's mind which they don't wish to share with others. Intentions are very important in psychic ability. So you want to hold the strong intention that you will only learn something about this person that they would feel good about you learning. You will intend to learn something about this person that you do not yet know. You will intend only good will for that person.

Speak a simple affirmation similar to this one:

> *I open myself to any information about this person (state their name) which he (or she) would feel comfortable with me knowing. I open myself to new information about this person. I have only good intentions for him (or her).*

This is a form of automatic writing.

First, look intently at the name or photo of the person that you are holding in your hand. Then you will start to continually scribble, draw or write on the paper. If you have the coordination to easily do so, continue to gaze at the person's name as you scribble, draw or write. But if that's too much to ask, turn your gaze to the paper upon which you are writing. Practice this for as long as you feel comfortable. When you are done, look at what you've drawn or written and analyze it to see if there is a message in it.

If you get a positive result from this, you may try this with other people. This is one way to make it real to you how all human minds are connected together.

But you should know that if you don't get any positive result from this, it is because there are still barriers which are blocking your psychic abilities. The next series of lessons teach you how to remove a major barrier to your psychic powers.

. Lesson Seven .

Gratitude bestows reverence, allowing us to encounter everyday epiphanies, those transcendent moments of awe that change forever how we experience life and the world.
John Milton

The Power of Gratitude

The biggest barrier to the development of your psychic powers are your feelings of ingratitude. This is because your feelings of ingratitude block your awareness of the Divine Source. If you are like most people, there are things in your life which you are unhappy about. When your attention is focused on these unhappy things in your life, you tend to ignore the many blessings that are always around you and within you. Of course you should try to change your life for the better, and the development of your psychic powers can help you to do that. But before you can do that, you need to learn to redirect your mental focus by developing persistent feelings of gratitude. I'm not talking about the *idea* of gratitude but the *feeling* of gratitude which you associate with the Divine Source of all existence. *This feeling of gratitude opens you to Divine Source Energy.*

There are two ways of viewing life; either you believe that

the world is a trap which curses all who have entered into it, or you believe that life is a blessing for which you are grateful. If you believe the latter, you have the potential to develop a high degree of psychic power. But if you actually believe that life is a trap which curses you, unless you're willing to change your attitude, it would be best if you didn't attempt to develop your psychic abilities. This is because in order to use your psychic powers ethically and effectively they must be founded on feelings of love and gratitude.

The Divine Source is the spiritual wellspring from which all existence emanates. To become fully accepting of the Divine Source Energy, you must feel grateful to the Divine Source. Most people do feel grateful for life. It may seem odd to you that there would be people who don't, but actually there are philosophical belief systems in which the creator of the world is viewed as being evil. Some occultists are members of secret societies which hold such beliefs. And they teach that the world is evil. However, if you believe that the world is evil, this becomes self-fulfilling. Your perception of reality is shaped by your beliefs. If you perceive the world as evil, it will become so for you. But if you perceive the world as good, you are in a better position to make it so. Gratitude for the Divine Source's blessings can change your perception of the world, and thus it will change your experience of the world.

I suggest that you take a moment and consider the true nature of your personal belief system.

Do you feel that life is a trap which curses you, and therefore do you hate the Creator of this trap? Or do you feel grateful for your life?

There's no point in trying to develop your psychic abilities if you aren't grateful for life; this is because the foundation for the highest level of psychic power is built on a grateful appreciation for the Divine Source.

Some people who dabble with the occult try to develop psychic abilities while maintaining an attitude of ingratitude for life. Also, there are occultists who are in rebellion against God because they desire to be the ones in power. Irrational fear is the unseen foundation for this obsessive desire to be in control of life. When you are grateful for your life, you desire to be in harmony with life rather than in control over it. This irrational obsession to always be in control is the essence of occultism. Negative attitudes keep occultists from attaining the highest level of psychic ability. It results in them using their limited psychic powers in unethical ways. Psychic abilities should never be used to harm other people or oneself.

The ethical use of psychic abilities demands that you use them for the benefit of humanity as well as yourself. Divine Source Energy is life's essence. The Divine Source loves all creation. The Divine Source loves humanity. When you base the development of your psychic abilities on an attitude of love and gratitude, your psychic abilities will become consecrated so that they will benefit both yourself and humanity.

Anointed Savior: This is the aspect of the Divine Source that brings you back into harmony with the Divine Source when you have fallen out of harmony with the Divine Source. When you are in concordance with the Divine Source, you become receptive to Divine Source Energy. So the Anointed

Savior is the personification of grace which allows you to accept Divine Source Energy. Another way of saying this is the the Anointed Savior is a spiritual presence that brings you back to your true self when you've lost yourself.

Personally I believe that there is grace and power in the name of *Jesus Christ*. In Hebrew, Jesus is *Yeshua*. But for English speaking persons, the religious name for the Anointed Savior is Jesus.

In my experience with persons who are developing psychic powers, those persons who renounce Jesus Christ, especially in public, often times develop serious problems in life as a result of this. So I would strongly suggest that you not renounce Jesus Christ.

The name Jesus Christ is the Christian religious name for the Anointed Savior. But if you are presently uncomfortable using the name Jesus Christ in your prayers or affirmations, it is enough that you simply refer to this expression of the Divine Source as *Anointed Savior*.

If your spiritual viewpoint is one in which you are grateful for life, you can attune to the Divine Source in a positive way; if you tend toward atheism, but you feel grateful for life, you can attune to the Divine Source in a positive way, so long as you can conceive of a Divine Source for all creation. The important thing is that you have a feeling of gratitude for your life.

clairvoyance: this means *clear seeing*. This is another name for psychic ability. With *clairvoyance* you can use your intuition to lucidly perceive the truth of things.

When you don't feel gratitude, you are not seeing things clearly. Feelings of ingratitude for life block your ability of clairvoyance.

The best way to unblock your psychic powers is through gratitude; the following drill is based upon this principle. Here you will create a *gratitude-list*.

Training Practice

What you will do in this exercise is this, you will write down a long list of things you feel grateful for. When you are done writing, you will read that list out loud. You will spiritually direct this reading of the gratitude list to the Anointed Savior. Whatever way that you phrase the wording of this gratitude-list is acceptable as long as it is written with sincerity.

The theme of the list, in general terms, might be something like this: "I am grateful to be alive. I am grateful for my loved ones. I am grateful for my physical health. I am grateful for my prosperity. I am grateful for my abilities. I am grateful for my possessions. I am grateful for this world."

The longer the list, the better. And the more specific and detailed it is, the better as well. You might write down things like, "I am grateful for my dog. I am grateful for my bicycle."

But don't just list material objects. You might write things like, "I am grateful for my intellect. I am grateful for my loving feelings for my friends."

If you have trouble thinking about what you actually feel

grateful for, think about what you *should* feel grateful for. Think of those things, which if you lost them, you would miss. Are you grateful for your eyesight? Are you grateful for your sexual feelings? Are you grateful for your ability to walk? Are you grateful to have a place to sleep at night? Are you grateful to have food to eat? Are you grateful for the beauty of nature? Are you grateful for the air you breath? Are you grateful to have drinkable water? Are you grateful for your income?

You can read this list out loud when you are alone, or you can read it out loud when you are with your study partner. However, before you read this gratitude-list out loud, evoke your awareness of the Anointed Savior by reverently speaking a prayer or affirmation.

You should know that this reading of a gratitude list to the Anointed Savior is a type of spiritual ritual.

Traditional Prayer

Our Father who is in Heaven, holy is your name. Your Kingdom come, your will be done, on Earth as it is in Heaven. Give us this day our daily bread. And forgive us as we forgive others. And lead us not into temptation, but deliver us from evil. For yours is the power and glory forever. Verily.

Divine Source Affirmation

Divine Source, whose eternal name is sacred. May

your Divine Source Energy be expressed on Earth as it is in the Spiritual Realm. May we be receptive to your Divine Source Energy. And may we be gracious with others as the Anointed Savior is gracious with us. Inspire us to humble righteousness. For all glory and praise are yours. Truly.

The process of this training exercise is as follows:

1. Write an extensive list of everything for which you should be grateful.

2. Say a prayer or affirmation to evoke your awareness of the Anointed Savior.

3. Read the gratitude list quietly out loud, reflecting feelings of gratitude in your voice.

As you live your life, if you find yourself falling into an attitude of ingratitude, you can repeat this process described above. Do this as often as needed until you have a persistent feeling of gratitude for your life.

. Lesson Eight .

The heart's memory eliminates the bad and magnifies the good. What matters in life is not what happened to you but what you remember and how you remember it.
                                    Gabriel Garcia Marquez

Attunement with the Divine

Psychic development primarily emerges from three things: training practices, spiritual rituals and spiritual insights.

Some of the training practices in this handbook are themselves spiritual rituals. Attunements are necessary to these spiritual rituals. To attune yourself to something is to bring yourself into harmonic awareness with something. Gratitude for life is the way to attune yourself to the Divine Source. However, disharmony with the Divine Source distorts all psychic abilities.

Clairvoyance means clear seeing. When you view the world with an attitude of ingratitude, then you aren't seeing the world clearly. When you view the world with an attitude of gratitude, then you are seeing the world clearly, as the Anointed Savior intends you to. This is why performing training exercises which reinforce your feelings of gratitude are essential to psychic training.

It's true that the world is sometimes hard and that some events in this world are disturbing. It's true that there is a presence of supernatural fear in this world. But to become a skilled psychic, you must take the attitude that everything in this world is either a gift to you from the Divine Source or a potential lesson to be learned.

Training Practice

The purpose of this drill is to help you to achieve this proper attitude. You should perform this at least once, and preferably more than once. But no more than one time per day.

Begin an journal; in it you will describe in detail your memory of happy episodes from your life. This will be of events that have taken place in the past. They will only be happy events, and the further in your past that you go, the better. Think of this as type of personal autobiography. But you shouldn't try to create this in any type of sequential order.

Episodic memory is a memory of an event which you have experienced in the real world. In this drill you will recall an episodic memory of a happy event for which you feel grateful. You will then systematically write down everything you can easily recall about that event.

In writing in this journal, ask yourself these questions:
- What was the time or date of this episodic memory?
- What did I see, touch, taste, smell and hear?

- What were my physical actions in this episode?
- What is my recall of other people in this episode?
- What made this event a happy one?
- What makes me feel grateful for this experience?

Example:

I recall a time I went on a picnic with my family. It was during spring break in 1967. We went to Forest Park in downtown St. Louis, Missouri. We got there about one o'clock in the afternoon and left a couple of hours later. It was a fun experience and everyone was happy. My father and mother were there as well as a friend of mine from the neighborhood. We sat at the Pavilion and ate our lunch. I remember the smell of fried chicken. I recall the taste of coleslaw. I recall my mother's laughter. I recall the feeling of warmth from the sun and how I felt cooler in the shade. I remember the smell of pipe tobacco when a man sitting nearby smoked after we ate. I remember the green of the grass on the hill. I recall seeing children playing in the fountain. My friend and I threw a frisbee back and forth. I recall the feeling of running as we did this. I recall a playful dog running around trying to catch the frisbee. I remember the sound of his barking. I feel grateful for this memory because it was a time when I was with people I cared about and I felt happy. I thank God that I've been allowed to have such happy experiences in my life.

While you are still a in training to awaken your psychic powers, try doing this drill on a regular basis. This not only helps you to maintain an attitude of gratitude, it also trains your mind. It's a mental exercise that will make it easier to use your psychic powers. If you were training yourself to play baseball, you might practice hitting baseballs into a batter's cage. With this drill, you are practicing to focus your mental concentration toward a specific task. Later in the course, this increased concentration will serve you as you learn to use your psychic powers.

To reiterate: each time you do this training drill, recall a happy experience from your past and write down your analysis of your memory of that experience. This can be from your distant past or your recent past.

You can allow your study partner to read what you write, but you don't have to.

Don't censor yourself, don't judge your own happiness. Whatever happy experience you choose to write about is OK. However, whatever it is that you write down, express gratitude to the Divine Source for having allowed you to have this experience. Give thanks.

. Lesson Nine .

As child and teenager I was subjected to abuse from persons trained in the CIA's MK Ultra mind-control experiments. These experiments were far more extensive than what many people realize. My parents were not informed about what was being done to me, although another older relative did know about this. If you haven't heard of MK Ultra, you might briefly do some research into it.

There were some psychologists who had been a part of this program who came to feel guilty because of their involvement in it. So they began to work as therapists to help heal the victims of MK Ultra. They would eventual help me by bringing me into therapy with them. With their help, eventually I was able to recover from the abuse that I had been subjected to. I have written about these therapists in other books.

The reason I mention this here is that these therapists used, as their primary healing technique, the recall of happy memories. Rather than traumatizing their clients all over again by having them relive painful memories, they focused on having us recall happy memories. They did this in a structured way. This tended to heal us emotionally. When we became emotionally stronger as a result of this, we would find that we could recall and process the painful memories on our own.

I've told you this story to point out the healing power that comes from recalling happy memories. I'm not telling you that you should deny or suppress your unhappy memories. But even if your life has had sad experiences, you've also had happy ones. And focusing on your happy memories will empower you, whereas dwelling on your unhappy ones will only sadden you.

Memory and Gratitude

Memory is the essential mechanism through which knowledge is conveyed and utilized by the human mind.

There are different types of memory. There is *informational memory*, which comes about when you memorize any piece of data. Your phone number is informational memory. And facts that you were taught to memorize in school is informational memory. But this is different than *episodic memory*. When you experience a memory of an *episode* of your life, you are recalling an *episodic memory*.

But it's possible to confuse an episodic memory with imagination. When you combine imagination with the memory of an actual life experience this is called *confabulation*. Without having any conscious intention to misrepresent the facts, a person may confabulate by recalling a memory that has been distorted through mental confusion. A *confabulation* is an imaginary memory that is believed to be real.

To be fully mentally lucid you need to be able to discern the difference between true episodic memory and confabulation. Mental lucidity is essential to the development of clairvoyance. So working with memory is essential to psychic training. And there are training drills which can help you to do this.

Begin a practice of writing a gratitude journal in which you list those experiences you have had that day for which you feel grateful. As well as this, write down any important life lesson that you may have had that day. You don't have to do this every day, but during the time when you are training yourself to develop psychic abilities, you should try to do this as often as you conveniently can. At the end of a day, think back upon the day and recall everything you experienced for which you are grateful.

Do not, do not, do not write down anything for which you are ungrateful. Never express ingratitude to the Divine Source. If you had an unhappy experience which taught you something important about life, you may write down the life lesson you have learned.

But the focus of the list must be on the things you feel grateful for or important life lessons that you have learned. These may be small things in life for which you feel grateful. Quickly and succinctly make a list of things for which you are grateful and life lessons learned, things that you experienced that day.

The more often you work with memories, the easier it is to have a lucid recall of memory. So this training drill below is a form of mental training as well as a way to develop the attitude of gratitude.

So this training drill is a three part process:

1. Toward the end of the day, this day, look back and write down a list of things that you experienced this day for which you feel grateful, and any life-lessons you have learned.

2. Say a prayer or affirmation and read the list quietly out loud.

3. Thank the Divine Source for what you've experienced.

Keep what you've written down and periodically, when convenient, perform this drill above. Also periodically review your gratitude journal.

. Lesson Ten .

You have swept them away like a flood, they fall asleep; in the morning they are like grass which sprouts anew.
Psalm 90:5

attunement: *noun,* this refers to the act of psychically connecting to another person or entity. This would also refer to the rituals or affirmations which help you to make such a connection.

> *Note:* If you tune a radio to a radio signal, you are selecting a specific frequency which will allow the radio station to broadcast through your radio to you. Think of tuning the radio as an analogy. What we are suggesting is that you can become mentally attuned to the Divine Source. The way that you attune your mind to the Divine Source is with feelings of gratitude for life. Once you've learned to persistently attune your mind to the Divine Source, you can attune your mind to other people who believe in the Divine Source, and you can attune your mind to the angels who are loyal to the Divine Source. And all of this opens you to Divine Source Energy.

evoke: *verb,* the act of bringing something forth from inside yourself.

invoke: *verb,* the act of calling something forth, usually something outside of yourself such as a calling forth of an angel. However, the terms evoke and invoke are essentially interchangeable; both of them refer to bringing something forth.

> *If you fail to bring forth that which is within you, that which is within will destroy you. If you bring forth that which is within you, that which is within you will save you.*
>
> The Gospel of Thomas

spiritual body: *noun,* this is defined as your emotional sensitivity to your feelings of love and empathy. The spiritual body contains your soul which is the essential source of your consciousness. But the spiritual body is also a way of conceptualizing your emotional self. Your spiritual body is the incorporeal body created by the psyche. Your spiritual body is your psyche's conception of self. Simply put, if the psyche can be thought of as having a form, the spiritual body is that form. *Your spiritual body is your superconscious mind.*

> ***Commentary:*** Some remote viewers that I have known have become so adept at remote viewing that they have been able to accurately observe the reality of other worlds in other star systems. Some psychics have the means to psychically observe the process by which a spiritual body reincarnates after death. These remote viewers and psychics have come to these conclusions based on such research. After the death of your physical body your spiritual body will continue to exist; if you are not yet in full

concordance with the Divine Source, your spiritual body will reconnect with a new physical body on this or some other world in the material universe. If you are in extreme discordance with the Divine Source when your physical body dies, you will reincarnate into unfavorable circumstances. If you are in partial harmonic concordance with the Divine Source, you will reincarnate under favorable circumstances after your physical body dies. If you are in perfect harmonic concordance with the Divine Source when your physical body dies, you will reincarnate into Heaven. This is a paradise reality which exists on a higher spiritual dimension. So once you incarnate into highest Heaven, you will become freed from the cycle of death, birth and reincarnation. But sometimes a psyche is traumatized by life and resists the process of reincarnation. When a spiritual body refuses to move on to its next incarnation, it may become a ghost for a time; but this is an undesirable condition, and most ghosts do eventually move on of their own accord.

gilgul: There is a Hebrew word *gilgul* which means "the wheel of souls" and this refers to reincarnation. This conception of reincarnation is not exactly the same as how Hindus, Buddhists or New Agers might conceive of reincarnation. Jews living in the time of Jesus, and many early Christians, believed in this doctrine of possible reincarnation. Grass is a perennial plant that dies in the winter and comes back in the spring. The Bible says, "All flesh is grass." Some have taken this as a reference to reincarnation. The idea of gilgul is that God may sometimes send a sainted soul back to reincarnate on Earth from Heaven during a time of humanity's need; this is why some early followers of Jesus asked if he were the reincarnation of certain prophets. *(Of course he was more than that.)* But this Hebrew idea of reincarnation also contained the belief that some souls, who were not good enough for Heaven but not evil enough for hell, might reincarnate into the world until the balance of their sinfulness or righteousness tipped in one direction or the other.

Your Personal Beliefs Concerning the Afterlife?

This training system for psychic development is not a religion, so there is no doctrine on the subject of life after death which you must accept. The Commentary above and the reference to gilgul may give you something to contemplate, but you don't have to accept this Commentary or a belief in reincarnation in order to develop your psychic abilities. Yet it is important to resolve the issue of what happens in the afterlife. Everyone must find peace of mind concerning their own eventual demise. Perhaps you should consult your own inner wisdom.

The training drill for this lesson is for you to redo the technique for automatic writing that you practiced in Lesson Four.

If you have done all of the preceding training drills in all of the preceding lessons you will have removed some blocks to your ability to receive psychic information. Perhaps you are ready to accept the wisdom which comes directly from your own inner divinity. The divine essence is in everyone if only they awaken to it. If necessary, reread the description of automatic writing found Lesson Four now.

Then ask your inner wisdom to send you insight into the nature of the afterlife through automatic writing.

. LESSON ELEVEN .

Science investigates, religion interprets. Science gives man knowledge, which is power; religion gives man wisdom, which is control. Science deals mainly with facts; religion deals mainly with values. The two are not rivals.
                                    Reverend Martin Luther King Jr.

Rejecting the Cult of Scientism

In the future, psychic technologies will tend to displace theology. This handbook that you are now reading is only one of many psychic technology systems that will develop in this new era of civilization. This emerging Age that we now find ourselves in is being created by a development in both spirituality and the sciences. Nonetheless, any psychic technology without empathic love would destructive to both the individual and society.

In the first place you must appreciate the difference between real science and *scientism*. Much of what passes as science is merely scientism. Real science refers to the empirical process and the data acquired from it; scientism is merely the opinions of persons who have identified themselves as being scientific. In other words, *scientism* is the unproven opinions of prestigious scientists; science itself is verifiable facts created by the empirical process.

The word *empiric* is based on a Greek root word for experiment. The empirical process is the method of creating reliable facts based on precise observation and verification through scientific experiments. The collection of these reliable facts becomes the basis of science. The application of scientific data becomes the basis of technology.

The think tank that developed these psychic training exercises studied a great deal of scientific data and developed these training techniques through a process of trial and error. So an empirical process was used in developing this system here.

But it must be acknowledged that there are limits to empirical science. This is because you have to appreciate that there is a difference between truth and data. Data is merely a collection of facts. Truth is the meaning that can be construed from the data.

Truth transcends the limits of science because science is confined to logic. Truth requires the interplay of logic and intuition. Those who have sought to apprehend the truth of anything with pure logic have always failed. The human mind just doesn't work that way.

There was a scientist named Kurt Godel who was fascinated with logic; however he eventually developed theorems which proved the futility of searching for pure logic. So you could consider that science itself has proven that there is no such thing as pure logic. Even common sense should tell you that human beings figure out the truth of things by using both logic and intuition.

But there have always been dishonest scientists who pretend that, because they are scientists, any idea they believe to be true must therefore be accepted as science. However, the intuition of a scientist is no better than the intuition of a non-scientist. Furthermore, contemporary training in the university system tends to suppress intuitive abilities so that the intuition of the average university-trained scientist is stunted. Therefore the opinions of scientists are often less scientifically valid than what they might suppose. In contemporary society, certain scientists set themselves up as authority figures in the minds of the public so that any opinion they express, no matter how wrong-minded, is nonetheless confused for real science. This is mere scientism.

Many of the devotees of the cult of scientism deny the truth of psychic ability in the name of *skepticism*. However I have found that these so-called skeptics are not very skeptical of their own preconceived notions, which assume the non-existence of psychic power in spite of much evidence.

Contemporary scientists in the university system tend to deny the validity of psychic ability because they have been covertly brainwashed by the educational system. Authentic freedom of thought is not possible in the pursuit of a university degree. The university system does teach people useful skills, but at the same time it programs them to deny certain truths. Contemporary scientific education is not the noble pursuit of truth that it pretends to be. It's really more of a system for training future corporate employees.

If you have made personal sacrifices and amassed a substantial student loan debt in the pursuit of higher education, you might feel offended at my seemingly unfair dismissal of university training. But know that I spent my four years in college, for what that was worth. I'm not disrespecting your university degree, if you have one, I'm just pointing out that university education will not help you, and may hinder you, in your development of psychic ability. You must learn to ignore this contemporary cult of scientism if you are to fully develop your psychic powers.

Psychic Education

A psychic is someone whose core identity is the spiritual body itself. A *psychic practitioner* is a self-actualized human being who is fully attuned to his or her spiritual body. This book represents a course. And this course does lead to certain specific abilities. In the process of studying in this course, you may become a skilled psychic practitioner.

The psyche is the unity of soul and mind. The spiritual body is the invisible form which the psyche takes. *In this book the soul is defined as the immortal and spiritual viewpoint of individual consciousness.* The mind is defined as subjective thoughts and emotions; the mind is the means through which the soul observes reality. When the physical body takes in information about the environment through the sensory organs, the mind is what processes this sensory information so that it can be apprehended by the soul's awareness. The mind takes sensory information and organizes it into a virtual-reality model of the environment. And the soul is the focus of consciousness which experiences this virtual-reality created by the mind.

Sensory perception is a process by which the body gathers sensory data. The mind organizes that data into a comprehensible model of reality. And the soul experiences that model of reality.

The mind has two aspects, there is the incorporeal mind of the spiritual body and the corporeal mind of the physical body; this corporeal mind is the brain's functions. The brain is an organic mechanism which operates on the basis of electrochemical interactions. The brain represents the mortal aspect of the mind, but the mind itself has aspects that transcend the brain. The transcendental aspect of an individual's mind is a personal energy field which interacts with the physical body through the brain and nervous system. This personal energy field is the mental aspect of the psyche, and it's generated by the focus of consciousness arising from the soul.

So a basic maxim for psychics is that consciousness creates mind, and that mind directs the flesh.

This truth is in opposition to the belief system of scientism which falsely assumes that the brain generates consciousness as some type of by-product of neural activity.

The truth is that the brain itself is not the generator of consciousness but the by-product of consciousness. If this truth seems illogical or counter-intuitive to you now, continue on with your studies and it may make sense.

The soul manifests the individual consciousness which illuminates the immortal aspect of the mind which is the spiritual body. It's through this spiritual body's interactions with tangible mental energies that the brain is programmed. The self is made up of soul, mind and physical body. The mind's tangible energies involve the spiritual body with the brain's functions which then operate the physical body.

To be a psychic practitioner isn't to deny the flesh, but to put the physical body into its proper perspective as it relates to the spiritual body. There is a shift in identity that takes place as a psychic novice evolves into a skilled psychic practitioner. The mundane individual identifies with the physical body, the psychic has the experience of knowing that he or she is the spiritual body which operates the physical body. During training, the typical novice starts off feeling that he or she is a physical body; but the awakened psychic ends up knowing, through experience, that he or she is a spiritual body.

Although your spiritual body is using your physical body for the purposes of sensory perception and physical action, your spiritual body can directly perceive reality without the physical body's help. Sensory perception is necessary in operating the physical body, but the spiritual body has every form of perception the physical body has as well as having other forms of perception.

When you learn to consciously use your spiritual body to directly perceive reality you become capable of extrasensory perception. Another way of explaining this would be to say that when you feel love for everything, you spiritually perceive everything with love.

However, while your physical body is alive, it is a sensory organ for your spiritual body. Your entire physical body receives and transmits vibratory psychic information. Your five sensory perceptions are sight, sound, touch, taste and smell. Your sixth sense is your extrasensory perception. The organ of perception for your sixth sense is your entire physical body. Your spiritual body thrives on your emotional sensitivity. When you are emotionally sensitive to the feelings that are within your physical body, you are opened to psychic information. Remember that your physical body is a gift given to you by the Divine Source. You can use this gift to transcendentally perceive the cosmos itself. But it is that internal quality of consciousness and emotional sensitivity which matters most. Your essential consciousness matters more than your physical body. And your essential consciousness does not have to be limited by the sensory-based model of reality produced by the brain.

Sensory perception is always an illusion because you don't experience your sensory perceptions directly. Your sense organs feed information to the brain on a real-time basis. Your brain has created a virtual reality, model of the real world, which is what you are experiencing now. This virtual reality system is continually updated, so it's easy to believe that you're directly perceiving the world with your senses. But if that were the case, how is it that anyone could see a hallucination?

Training Practice of Mirror Gazing

This technique is to be practiced only one time, and you should practice it for a relatively short period of time. This probably won't take more than fifteen minutes. The purpose of this drill is to allow you to recognize that the model of reality, created by the brain's interpretation of sensory input, is not a direct perception of reality. Right now, look at the ground or floor beneath your feet. What you are really seeing is a neural construct created by the brain. You are not actually looking at the floor. However you might say that it looks real enough. OK. So try this. Find a mirror. Stand or sit perfectly still. Gaze at the mirror, blinking your eyes only as necessary. Make eye contact with your mirror image and continue to focus there. What you will probably observe if you do this long enough is a distortion of your mirror reflection. This may make it apparent to you that what you're seeing is really just a construct created in your brain. Try this now.

. Lesson Twelve .

*To see a World in a grain of sand
And Heaven in a Wild Flower,
Hold Infinity in the palm of your hand
And Eternity in an hour.*

William Blake

material universe: *noun,* this is the matter, energy and space acting through time which comprises the universe that you can observe with your sensory perceptions. This is the universe which you can touch, taste, smell, hear and see. The material universe is made up of tangible things such as electromagnetic energy and basic elements. Your physical body is a part of the material universe.

precognition: This is the ability to know the future before it occurs. There are three types of future events that may be perceived: those written in sand, those written in clay and those written in stone. This is a metaphor. Sand = events easily changed. Clay = events that can be changed with effort. Stone = events that can't be changed.

subatomic: *adjective,* describes something which has dimensions smaller than that of an atom. Subatomic forces too small to be measured with the instruments of science are the foundational building blocks of the universe.

sentient being: *noun*, any being which is intelligent to the point of being self aware. This would include all human beings, angels and intelligent extraterrestrial beings. To varying degrees of intensity, animal life forms are also sentient.

Like Waves on the Ocean

Consciousness is the greatest power in the universe, and it is the foundation of all subatomic forces in the universe. All forms of energy and matter arise from the subatomic level of the universe, formed by the intelligence of the Spiritual Realm. As well as having a material form, the cosmos itself manifests the qualities of consciousness and intelligence. This is an understanding which some of the most advanced thinkers in quantum physics have realized.

The word *quantum* come from the same root word as quantity. These quantum particles are subatomic expressions of energy. When I read about quantum particles, I can't help but to think of waves in the ocean. An ocean wave is a temporary identifiable form, but it's never really a separate entity from the ocean. An ocean wave is identifiable as such, but it isn't a discrete entity, separate from the ocean. When I hear physicists talk about quantum particles, I sometimes wonder if they can be thought of as being truly discrete. Perhaps like waves on the ocean, quantum particles periodically arise from the great sea of cosmic consciousness.

The natural laws that govern these subatomic particles do

seem to defy traditional scientific analysis. You don't need to understand physics to become psychic, but you do need to understand consciousness. I point all this out because some quantum physicists have become open to the idea that consciousness is an essential quality of the cosmos itself.

Deconstructing the Mechanical Universe

However, scientists have not always embraced the idea that the essential foundation of the universe is consciousness.

The early scientists, the natural philosophers, like Rene Descartes and Isaac Newton, tended to envision the universe as a giant clockwork machine. Intellectuals in post-medieval Europe would come to embrace this idea. The large mechanical clocks, that had become popular in Europe in those days, became a metaphor which they used to describe the entire universe. Over time, this metaphor of the mechanical clock as the universe became more than a mere metaphor, it evolved into a schematic description of the universe. In other words, it became a conceptual model for the universe. So in the minds of these early scientists, this mechanical model for reality was born.

Charles Darwin would come along in 1859 and apply this mechanical model to biology in describing evolution as a mechanical process.

He sold this idea to the world:

> *In every species there are always some who have slight genetic mutations. Some are taller, some*

smaller, some birds with larger beaks and so forth. When the environment changes, some mutations are more adaptable to the new environment, and thus they are more likely to survive and reproduce. Eventually, over extremely long periods of time, that particular type of mutation becomes the norm, and thus the species has changed; it has become taller, smaller, has a larger beak or whatever.

This was Darwin's mechanical theory of *Natural Selection*.

In Darwin's description of evolution there is no place for any consciousness to guide Natural Selection; for Darwin there was no place for an intelligent-designer of life. Darwin completely embraced the idea that life arose from chemical processes and then proceed to evolve into new forms through a mechanical process of Natural Selection, which took place over very long periods of time. Darwin's theory of Natural Selection is devoid of any moral authority. According to his theory, the life forms which survive to reproduce themselves do so because of an amoral tendency to be more rigorous or adaptable than other life forms. In the Darwinian world view, all life forms compete with one another in the brutal struggle for survival.

Almost immediately, Darwin's mechanical process of evolution became the basis of *Social Darwinism*. This philosophy put forward the idea that the amoral struggle for survival is some type of higher virtue so that all of society should be based on brutal competition. Social Darwinism became the basis for justifying the viewpoint that the strong *should* exploit the weak. This means that strong nations could justify invading weaker nations and that wealthy persons could justify exploiting the poor. Under various different names, Social Darwinism became a basic world view which the leaders of the Industrial Revolution adopted. So this mechanical model of reality came to dominate the mind set of modern society; and as the Industrial Revolution spread to the entire world, this mechanical model of reality became the dominant paradigm for the global community.

One materialistic philosopher took this type of thinking so far as to make fun of the idea of the human soul, saying that it was nothing but a ghost in the machine.

However this *mechanical model of reality* was never anything but a metaphor. And just as a map is not the territory it describes, a metaphor is merely a way of describing reality, it's not reality itself. Back in the days of Newton, the mechanical clockwork model may have been a good metaphor for the universe. But as science progressed, this metaphor proved to be overly simplistic and inaccurate.

With time, this mechanical model for reality was shattered by the ideas of Albert Einstein and the other scientific pioneers of quantum physics. As they studied the structure and function of the atom, these advanced scientific thinkers came to realize that the classical, mechanical view of reality was not the authentic basis for the universe. Advanced quantum physics indicates a relationship between consciousness and subatomic particles, and thereby atomic structure. Those things that we can see and touch are what we call matter.

Matter is made up of compounds which are made up of basic elements which are made up of atoms which are made up of subatomic forces.

The atomic building blocks of matter are actually energetic forces. In other words, an atom is a submicroscopic structured field of energies. The components of an atom arise from subatomic forces. And what many of the most advanced scientists have realized is that at a foundational level of the universe, subatomic forces demonstrate the qualities of consciousness. Therefore, consciousness isn't a unique quality of the human brain, but rather consciousness is an intrinsic aspect of the entire cosmos.

So we are not ghosts trapped in a giant universal machine; we are living beings interacting with living energies within a living cosmos.

Social Darwinism has proven to be a morally bankrupted philosophy. It has resulted in a type of deep corruption of society which now threatens to destroy all civilization.

The philosophical basis of Social Darwinism was the Darwinian biology of the 1800s. However, modern biology has shown that Darwin's ideas were presumptuous. He formed his theory of evolution prior to discoveries concerning DNA and the complex functioning of cellular components.

Anyone who understands the sophistication of a single strand of DNA found in a gene knows that it could not have come about through an accidental chemical reaction. This would be as if the forces of nature accidentally created a subcellular super-computer far more advanced than any of our contemporary nanotechnology.

Furthermore, some cellular components have irreducible complexity; irreducible complexity means that you can't add or take away even a single molecule necessary to the cellular component or it won't function; in other words, there is no room for mutations, therefore Natural Selection could not have generated these cellular components; what this means is they're intelligently-designed organic machines which can't be explained with Darwin's theory.

Put simply, Darwin's mechanical view of biology was wrong. It has been proven wrong a thousand times in a thousand ways. Yet the high priests of scientism still cling to its doctrine with the intensity of their cultic fanaticism.

Virtually everyone, including Darwin's critics, believe that an individual species can change form in an adaptation to its environment. And Darwin's observations in the Galapagos Islands demonstrated this very well. But even before Darwin came along, there were scientists who believed this. Anyone can see that dogs and horses are influenced by their breeding. It makes common sense that individual species adapt themselves to their environment over many generations.

Darwinism is the belief that one species can adapt itself until it turns into a completely different species. So that given incredibly long periods of time, over many generations, monkey-like primates evolve into humans. It is also the belief that life came into being through some chemical process of nature: perhaps lighting striking a brackish pond. So this is used to deny that there is a divine creator of life. The problem is that if you do enough hard research you will find that there really isn't any scientific proof for Darwinism. There's no proof in science that one species turns into another, this is all unproven speculation. There's no proof that life arose from chemical processes in nature. Darwinism is merely more scientism.

The argument made for Darwinism is that it is a *science-based* explanation for the origin of species, but actually it isn't. Many intellectuals in Darwin's time were interested in mysticism and esoteric philosophy. Darwin was known to attend seances with George Eliot. A German scholar named Friedrich Max Muller, famous for translating oriental esoteric doctrines, was in communication with Darwin for many years prior to Darwin's publication of the Origin of Species in 1859.

In these ancient philosophies, that Darwin was known to study, there was an esoteric belief in the evolution of one species to another. Fish gods turn into human gods, for example. In the Zodiac you see a creature that is half-goat and half-fish. There are many mythological creatures that are made up of different species.

A common theme of these esoteric doctrines is that of the *mineral body, plant body and animal body*, all of which represent different ages leading up to the age of *man*. In esoteric symbolism you find Darwin's basic theory: which is that, over long periods of time, minerals evolve into plants which evolve into animals which evolve into humans.

Frank Baum, who wrote *The Wizard of OZ*, was once a student of the philosophies of the Rosicrucian religion and Theosophy which reference this esoteric idea of the four ages of mineral, plant life, animal and man. He humorously ridiculed these esoteric ideas with the four characters of Tin Man (mineral), Straw Man (plant), Cowardly Lion (animal) and Dorothy (human). The real joke is on anyone who doesn't realize that Darwinism itself never originated out of a desire for pure scientific truth.

Darwinism isn't a science-based theory at all. It's an ancient religious esoteric belief presented with a *pseudoscientific* explanation by Darwin. Yet it is still taught in schools as if it were science. And worse than that, it is used to suppress real science.

There are good reasons, based on real science, to believe that there is an *intelligent designer* of life. The Divine Source is real. We don't live in an accidental universe. Life on Earth and humanity are not some cosmic mistake that came about through unconscious mechanical processes.

Furthermore, it's wrong to say that life is driven by competition. Although competition does take place between species, it's the cooperation of symbiotic life forms which most enhances survival. Furthermore, in terms of society, it's the cooperation of human beings with one another which most strengthens civilization. It's cooperation, not competition, which is the foremost dynamic which enhances survival, whether that be biological survival or the survival of a human civilization.

Social Darwinism with its endorsement of amorality is nothing but a pseudo-intellectual justification for insanity and criminality.

Both Darwinism and Social Darwinism are examples of the harm that is caused by scientism.

You must come to fully appreciate the difference between science and scientism. Real science is nothing more than a collection of facts. These facts have been produced through an empirical system. These scientific facts can be used to create useful technologies. But what they can't really do is to create an accurate model of reality for life or the universe. Science is a useful tool but a poor basis for philosophy. Just because a scientist expresses a belief, does not make that belief into a scientific fact. Scientism is the worship of science as if it were a god. In this distorted view of science, any opinion expressed by a prominent scientist, or a group of prominent scientists, is accepted as if it were a self evident truth.

Although it is a fact of science to say that Darwin's theory of Natural Selection might explain how an individual species can adapt itself to its environment by changing form, it's scientism to say that Darwin's theory proves the biological evolution of one species into another, or that it can be applied in any way to human society.

Furthermore, it's actually possible that the mechanical process of Natural Selection may have nothing to do with how a species changes form to adapt itself to its environment. Perhaps the all knowing Divine Source continually uses Divine Source Energy to program the DNA of the various species so as to adapt them better to their changing environment. In other words, God is willing these adaptations to take place, and Natural Selection has nothing to do with it. There may be no empirical evidence for this theory of the *continual Divine-influencing* of all the species, but then again, there is no empirical evidence for Darwinism either.

The mechanical model of reality, that was so cherished by the early scientists, has been proven to be an overly simplistic philosophy which simply is not true. Yet in spite of the proof otherwise, many contemporary scientists are still prisoners of the mechanical universe, but to develop your psychic abilities you need to transcend all that nonsense. If you wish to awaken your psychic abilities, you must escape the psychological prison of this mechanical universe.

The Power of Directed Awareness

You need to realize that your ability to consciously direct the focus your mind is the key to all psychic ability. This cannot be emphasized enough. Consciousness is the foundation of all energy in the universe, and energy is the foundation for all matter. As many have said, where your attention goes, your energy flows. Your qualities of consciousness and intelligence are transformational in changing the universe. And you don't need advanced training to practice *telekinesis*; this is the ability for your mind to directly influence matter through a spiritual means; most people just fail to realize that they have this power. Simple prayer can be a subtle expression of telekinesis.

For example, as a psychic you can learn to direct your consciousness in such a way so as to stimulate the healing process in a person who is on the other side of the world. And in this process of remotely healing another person, you will have no direct contact with that person, you will only be using your mental concentration. But in using your mental concentration alone, you will be able to physically heal someone located in a remote environment, far away from you. Even without advanced training in psychic remote healing, if you pray for another person who is ill, that act will subtly stimulate physical healing in that person even if he or she is located in a remote location. You may not be able to lift inanimate objects with your mind, but you can stimulate healing in yourself and others. And that's even more important.

In using psychic abilities, distance makes no difference because pure consciousness can instantly transverse any distance. This is something that Descartes with his clockwork mechanical model of the universe could never have understood. To awaken your psychic powers, you must make a quantum leap and abandon the old fashion thinking of anyone who still clings to this outmoded mechanical paradigm. I have even heard some contemporary scientists say that the whole concept of consciousness is irrelevant because they can't prove it empirically. That type of thinking is a trap which negates the development of psychic ability. You must simply leave behind those who choose to remain in this trap and move forward into freedom.

Your quality of awareness is the essence of your personal power. To be fully human is to be aware of your free will, your emotions, your thoughts and your actions in the present moment. To deny this quality of consciousness is to deny your humanity as well as your potential for psychic power.

In becoming a psychic practitioner you learn to discipline your mind so that you can release the transformational power of your consciousness. And one important step in doing this is to learn to direct your attention upon a single point of concentration. You cannot learn to concentrate on sending healing psychic energy to a person on the other side of the world until you can learn to concentrate upon the perception of something in your immediate environment.

Training Practice

The psychic exercise for this lesson is that of mental concentration. There is a technique used in many different systems of meditation training. This is called *candle gazing*. The training system in this handbook expresses its own unique version of this technique. To do this you will sit comfortably in a chair where you can gaze upon a lit candle that is set upon a table before you. You will then make an application of the process of *psychic scanning* which uses the method of *scan, subvocalize and cognize*.

So this practice has three basic steps.

- Step One: **SCAN**

In order to learn to make a psychic scan, you need to first learn to scan with your intellect and emotions. When you visually scan the contents in a room in looking for a particular object, you are using your sensory perception of eyesight. But even in such a case a small degree of intuition comes into play. In this training drill of candle gazing, you are scanning your own body with your feelings. You simply place your attention on the feelings of stress that you are holding in your physical body. This too is another step in your psychic training. Through the repeated use of this type of scanning, you will slowly awaken your natural ability to make psychic scans by using your emotions.

For this practice, you will first scan your physical body for tension. In this scan, do a systematic analysis of where you are holding unnecessary tension in your body. Start with your toes and move your attention upward until you reach your scalp. Look for any tension in your muscles or in your breathing. When you feel any such stress being held in your body, you will intentionally relax, letting go of the tension.

- Step Two: **SUBVOCALIZE**

After you have relaxed your physical body during this brief scan, you then go into a subvocalization of a memorized invocation. Listed below are two examples of invocations that you may use for this. One invocation is religious and the other is non-religious, so you have a choice. Or you can choose an appropriate invocation of your own. Read and reread one of these listed invocations until you have memorized it. You will learn to subvocalize this invocation to bring into your mind an awareness of the Divine Source Energy.

Religious Invocation

> The light of God surrounds us,
> The love of God enfolds us,
> The power of God protects us,
> The presence of God watches over us,
> Wherever we are, God is.

Non-Religious Invocation

> The light of love surrounds us,
> The aura of love enfolds us,
> The power of love protects us,
> The presence of love watches over us,
> Wherever we are, love is.

- Step Three: **COGNIZE**

Having invoked this spiritual awareness through a subvocalized invocation, you then gaze gently at the hypnotic candle flame. Blink as necessary, relax naturally and breathe normally. In this silence you will feel aware of the Divine Source Energy. In doing this you will use your emotional sensitivity to cognize (realize) your relationship with the Divine Source. Such cognitions may not be ideas so much as they are feelings of love. The Divine Source loves you unconditionally, and when you focus upon your awareness of Divine Source Energy you may come to know that love. Your awareness of the unconditional love of the Divine Source may be your cognition. But some people may have an intellectual response to this practice. It may happen that other thoughts will occur to you about your relationship with the Divine Source. So the cognition may be purely emotional, purely intellectual or a combination of emotion with intellect.

So to put this simply: while sitting and gazing at a candle flame you will first focus your attention upon relaxing your body, then you will subvocalize a prayer or affirmation and finally you will let your thoughts go where they will. But if you lose your feeling of serenity, repeat the above described three part process as needed.

However, no matter what the response is, after you subvocalize the invocation, you will have a psychic response of some kind. This may not be an earthshaking response, it probably will be something subtle. And at first you might not sense anything at all. However, even if you don't sense anything, keep your attention focused upon the candle flame.

Light is a symbol for the Divine Source. Divine Source Energy is an invisible source of inner illumination. Christ said that he was the light of the world. In all philosophies around the world light has been used as a symbol of spiritual awakening. Although the Divine Source Energy is invisible, the light of the candle gives you a tangible form to gently gaze upon.

Don't glare intensely at the flame, blink as necessary and let your gaze become unfocused so that you feel comfortable. As long as your attention is focused upon the flame, your mind is open to Divine Source Energy. As you master this practice you will find that you do have a serene response of some kind.

- Repeat the Steps: **SCAN / SUBVOCALIZE / COGNIZE**

As you mentally focus in silence upon the Divine Source Energy, other mundane thoughts may come into your attention to distract you. Instead of just having spiritual realizations about the nature of your relationship with the Divine Source, you may find yourself distracted by thoughts of ordinary mundane life. These might be concerns or desires related to your everyday life, things like your worries about bills or wondering what you're going to eat for lunch. When this type of distraction happens, which it will, simply imagine that those mundane thoughts are burnt away by the flame of the candle. Then you go back to a new cycle of the process of scan/subvocalize/cognize.

Each session candle gazing need only last ten to fifteen minutes. However, the more times that you do this, the more you will become aware of your feeling for the Divine Source

Energy. You will have stronger and stronger feelings for this spiritual presence with practice. Don't worry if your feeling for this spiritual presence is weak at first. You are performing an act of faith every time you perform this process.

To reiterate, the three parts of this mediation technique are the scanning for relaxation, subvocalizing the invocation, and knowing the spiritual presence of the Divine Source Energy as you gaze at the light of a candle. After a minute or so of gazing serenely at the candle flame, if you want to, you can repeat the scan of your body for tension, repeat the invocation and return to the serene feelings that you experience as you gaze at the candle flame.

You may find that while you are in this process of scan, subvocalize and cognize you will fall into a deep state of open-eyed meditation where you let go of conscious thought and experience a happy serenity. This can be a good thing.

This practice of candle flame gazing is a spiritual ritual in which you attune yourself to the Divine Source Energy. It's through such acts of faith that you increase your spiritual connection with the Divine Source.

This practice serves several purposes. It is a mental exercise in which you are disciplining your thoughts. This exercise helps in teaching you psychic scanning. It helps in conditioning yourself to be able to go easily into a state of relaxation at will. It helps in training yourself to remain centered in the present moment. And it helps in training you to hold your concentration on a single point of mental focus for extended periods of time.

This training exercise may also be used as an ongoing practice. You should practice this on an regular basis for as long as you are developing your psychic powers through training, and perhaps even after you've become awakened to you psychic powers. The more times you use this practice the more you will find that you spend an increasing amount of time in periods of deep meditation. In such periods of deep meditation, you feel the Divine Source Energy without any mundane thoughts which might distract you. With time, your awareness of this spiritual presence will become stronger. As a psychic you will be able to learn how to use this connection in the advanced practices.

One thing which can interfere with the success of this practice is the intrusion of the ego. The ego is the aspect of your personality which identifies itself as the physical body. Because you aren't really your physical body, the ego is to some extent based upon an illusion. But this illusion is necessary for physical survival. So you do need your ego. But it is your ego which is the source of your mundane thoughts.

Candle gazing is used to transcend mundane thinking. You stop the mental chatter of your mundane thoughts so you can take time to feel and know a spiritual presence. The ego is a necessary component of a healthy self image. The ego is not evil, but it can be a kind of monkey-mind in that it sometimes chatters away like a monkey. Even when you try to quiet your mind, so that you can feel the Divine Source Energy, this monkey-mind of the ego will want to chatter on. It may repeat songs in your mind that you've heard earlier on the radio. It may focus in on arguments that you've had in the past. It may focus in on unfulfilled materialistic desires.

Some of these ego-driven thoughts may at times seem quite fascinating. You may want to cling to some of these mundane thoughts. Sometimes it may be difficult to discern which thoughts are coming from the ego and which may be arising from the Divine Source. However, the ego is concerned with mundane things, not your spiritual relationship with the Divine Source.

This is how you discern ego-driven thoughts from spiritual cognitions; you must know the difference between the mundane and the spiritual. And such discernment arises from feelings of serenity. Those thoughts which move you deeper into serenity are spiritual, but those thoughts which move your attention away from serenity are mundane.

Of course, the ideal state for this meditation experience is one in which you don't think anything at all but merely feel serenity. It's in such feelings of serenity that you know (cognize) the true nature of the Divine Source.

However, if you become fascinated with distracting, mundane thoughts, you will miss the point of this practice. It's only natural to worry about how you are going to pay the bills or what you are going to eat for lunch. You're not a bad person because such ego-driven thoughts do come up. It's better to just acknowledge these thoughts when they enter into your awareness, then imagine these distracting thoughts as being burnt away by the candle flame, then subvocalize the invocation once again, and then return to the knowing the spiritual presence of the Divine Source Energy.

The reason this simple practice is important is that invoking the Divine Source Energy is the starting point of many other psychic practices. So the time and effort you put into mastering this practice creates the foundation for more advanced skills. Furthermore, once you master this meditation technique it can be a source of spiritual joy.

. Lesson Thirteen .

Decades ago I quit smoking cigarettes. It's a good thing that I did because I probably wouldn't have survived this far if I hadn't. I only smoked ten cigarettes a day, but they clearly were diminishing my health. I tried several techniques for quitting, none of which worked. And every time I tried to quit cold turkey, I always started up again in a few days.

So I decided to use meditation.

In intervals of ten days, I decreased the number of cigarettes I smoked every day by one cigarette. So first I reduced my tobacco intake to nine cigarettes a day. After ten days of this, I reduced it to eight, and so on. After about three months of this slow reduction I was able to stop completely. I never returned to the habit of smoking again.

What made it possible for me to go through this slow process of nicotine withdrawal was that I practiced meditation for long periods of time every day. I significantly increased the amount of time that I spent in meditation during the period of withdrawal. So meditation ultimately saved my life.

ego: *noun,* in this handbook, the ego is defined as the ideas which you associate with the physical body. The ego is your identification of yourself as your physical form. The true self is the spiritual body, which is the spiritual focus point of consciousness. Arising from this focus point are thoughts and images, which comprise the mind. Through the brain, the mind relates itself with the physical body. The mind then dedicates itself to fulfilling the needs of the physical body. It's those ideas about the physical self which form the ego.

There is nothing bad about having an ego. You need to have an ego in order to survive. Brainwashing is an attack upon the individual's ego; and such practices are destructive to mental health. This system of psychic training doesn't require you to destroy your ego. If anything, it makes your ego healthier.

But when you become fixated on egotistical thoughts, you come to suppress psychic abilities. You need to be able to set your ego aside for a while in order to awaken psychic abilities.

In order to function as a person in society, you must normally act as if you believe yourself to be your body. For example, when a person accidentally cuts his finger, he might say, "I cut myself." It's normal to identify oneself as ones physical body. That identification is the ego.

Although the ego isn't really the true self, it's a necessary illusion. This illusion of ego makes operating the physical body possible. So the ego isn't evil, but it also isn't real. During moments of deep meditation and other spiritual experiences, you may rediscover that which is real. You experience that rediscovery in moments of serenity. More than anything else, you are the consciousness that resides in your feelings of serenity and love.

invocation: *noun,* in this handbook, an invocation is defined as a ritual, process, or set of affirmations which invokes a mutual awareness with another sentient being. Two telepaths, for example, could create a unique affirmation by which one could establish telepathic contact with the other when needed and that affirmation would be their telepathic invocation.

For example, let's say that two telepaths named Jane and John might make up a simple invocation phrase, "John and Jane are joined in mind." And whenever one wants to telepathically contact the other, he or she would repeat the phrase as a meditative subvocalization until he or she felt the other was receptive. Then John and Jane would telepathically transmit mental image pictures back and forth as a means of *remote communication* at a distance.

The most important invocation is one which connects you with the Divine Source Energy. Although you might say that the Divine Source is always aware of you, when you use an invocation you are bringing forth your own conscious connection to the Divine Source Energy. And you must do this of your own free will. The potential for this mental connection is always there. The invocation process is a mechanism of the intellect which affirms this connection. The Divine Source has gifted you with free will, and so you must affirm your receptiveness to Divine Source Energy of your own free will. So an invocation is any expression of this intention.

A Culture of Spiritual Deprivation

A psychic recognizes that the physical body is a source of pleasure to be enjoyed; however, a psychic values the pleasures of the spirit above the pleasures of the flesh. A psychic recognizes the value of physical health and the welfare of the physical body; however, the code of discipline of the psychic requires that the needs of the psyche are predominant over the desires of the physical body. A psychic appreciates an emotional sensitivity to the physical body; however, the psychic never allows feelings of fear, anger or hatred to emotionally hijack his or her behavior. Nevertheless, this attitude of spiritual predominance goes against the values of materialistic, mundane society.

Too often, in this present day culture, individuals allow the impulsive whims of their physical bodies to dictate their behavior. This is how people become addicted to drugs and self-destructive habits. Contemporary culture has become defined by addictive behaviors such as overeating, alcoholism, drug abuse, sexual perversions, greedy wealth-acquisition, hoarding, irrational violence and the obsessive use of media such as TV or video games. There are many ways that people can lose control of their lives to some type of addiction. But as a psychic, you must realize that behind every addiction is spiritual deprivation; what this means is that the human psyche itself has been suppressed by this culture of mundane materialism.

Self discipline is not the adherence to rules and regulations. The psyche is the true self. The psyche is the source of your thoughts, awareness and loving emotions. The psyche is your soul and mind. You are your psyche. You are spirit. Therefore self discipline is achieved when spiritual needs are valued over materialistic desires. Spiritual deprivation is overcome through enjoyable spiritual practices and the living of a happy spiritual lifestyle.

Yet the psyche can become suppressed through a number of means. Mind control, brainwashing, physical abuse and torture are some of the ways in which an individual can become disassociated. With the death of the physical body, the spiritual body disconnects completely from the physical vehicle. However, there are lesser traumas which do not result in such a complete disconnection. When the psyche is suppressed by the abuses of life, it can become somewhat separated from an emotional awareness of the physical body, it emotionally disconnects to some degree. This is called *disassociation*.

Emotions arise from the interplay of the spiritual body with the physical body. While in the human condition, for intuition to be effective, you must be sensitively connected to your emotions. Disassociation would take place if you allowed yourself to become emotionally desensitized.

When someone becomes persistently disassociated, spirituality ceases to be the prime motivator of that person's behavior. The physical body has its own instinctive drives, and when the psyche disassociates, those instinctive drives take over.

Your psyche is your emotional and thinking self. But if you were to experience too much emotional trauma or mental confusion, then your emotional sensitivity and rational thought processes would be decreased; such a condition would be the state of disassociation. When disassociation takes place, physical instincts hijack human behavior. This is how the spiritual body loses control of the physical body.

Although the instinctive drives of the physical body are there for survival, they can become warped by various environmental factors. There is the natural flight or fight response to the presence of a threat in the environment. When persons become too frightened they may lose touch with their powers of reason and behave irrationally when this fight or flight instinct hijacks their behavior. The dehumanizing social environment of contemporary society creates continual and overwhelming threats which have come to suppress the natural courage of human beings.

The brain and nervous system can stimulate the secretion of a certain type of hormone called *endorphins*, which influence the physical body in a number of ways. *Endorphins* are the brain's natural reward system for those behaviors that support survival. However, this *endorphin response* can also create problems for a person who is in a dehumanizing environment which encourages unnatural behavior. The brain produces endorphins which naturally create feelings of pleasure and well-being. Love making, eating a good meal, vigorous exercise, having a success in life: all these things can stimulate endorphin production in the brain. When done properly, spiritual experiences through prayer and meditation can also stimulate endorphins. All of these behaviors are good. However, drugs and compulsive behaviors can stimulate endorphins in unnatural ways. When the psyche becomes disassociated, then the behaviors of the physical body are instinctively drawn to drugs and compulsive behaviors as a means to stimulate endorphins. This tendency to create endorphins through these unnatural practices can degrade the individual's will power and cause him or her to lose control.

When people lose control over their lives they may find themselves trapped in a controlled environment such as a prison or drug treatment center. When addicts submit themselves to a drug treatment center, they're admitting that they've lost control over their lives. They're surrendering their freedom to the control of their therapists. However, this can have a positive influence if treatment is done correctly.

For example, a patient may come to realize that if somebody else can control his behavior, then he himself can take back control of his own behavior. However it can also happen that a patient might simply give up trying to control himself and instead become dependent upon an institution. Becoming chronically institutionalized in this way isn't an expression of self discipline; in fact it's the opposite of self discipline because it's the institution itself which is imposing the discipline.

This brings up the materialistic, mundane conception of self discipline. Mundane thinking persons tend to define self discipline as the acceptance of the control of an authority figure. However, in accepting the control of an authority figure, such as a drill sergeant, you may become disconnected from your own thoughts and feelings. This could become just more disassociation. Simply doing what someone in authority tells you to do doesn't make you self disciplined.

The essence of the self is the soul, mind, and physical body. The soul is essentially good; the soul is moral by nature. As well as that, the human mind is rational by nature. Furthermore, the physical body is naturally healthy. Human beings are naturally good.

But the physical body is vulnerable to torture and various forms of deprivation, such as starvation. Through continual stress, torture or deprivation, the physical body can be abused to cause mental illness. When the soul is suppressed and the mind is broken, then irrational human behavior may result. The natural goodness of a human being can be suppressed so that a person will come to think and behave in ways that seem evil. And contemporary society often does destroy the natural goodness of human beings.

A man may restrain himself from criminal violence because he's afraid of prison. In such a case he isn't expressing self discipline, he's repressing his violence impulses out of fear; so he's controlled by fear rather than self discipline. But if a man refrains from criminal violence because he feels empathy for others, then he's truly self disciplined.

Spiritual awareness is the key to empathy, and empathy is the key to moral behavior. When you feel empathy for others, you do unto others as you would have them do unto you. When you are aware of your empathy for others, you are expressing your authentic self.

Extending empathy to others is an expression of psychic ability. If you feel your empathic connection with another person strong enough, you will be able to read his or her mind. Telepathy is nothing more than a mental scanning technique which takes advantage of a strong empathic link with another person.

Think about how mothers often feel a natural telepathic connection to their new born infants. A mother can feel what's going on with her child although that child can't speak to her. Psychic abilities will result when you combine feelings of love with mental discipline. The most powerful psychics are also the most compassionate.

Mental and emotional health are essential to psychic development. This is one way in which an ethical psychic differs from the occult dabbler. Mentally ill people sometimes experiment with occult knowledge because they believe that they can use it to accomplish their worldly desires of lust, greed or revenge. The ethical psychic is above such indulgences. An ethical psychic desires to use his or her powers for good purposes. Although an ethical psychic may use these powers for self benefit, he or she also desires to be of service to humanity and life.

So the key to overcoming addictive behaviors and to achieving self discipline is the *healing of the psyche*. The psyche is strengthened by spiritual activities. The psyche is strengthened by the development of the mind. You don't become self disciplined by disconnecting from your thoughts and feelings, you become self disciplined by enhancing your sensitivity to your thoughts and feelings. Mundane thinking persons often fail to appreciate this point. As the mind and soul are strengthened, self discipline becomes natural. This is what it means to have control over your own life.

All of the lessons and practices described in this handbook

are designed to put you into control over your life. All of these lessons and practices enhance the proper relationship between the spiritual body and the physical body. Ethical psychic development requires self discipline. But this type of self discipline should be a joy, not a boring chore. The ethical psychic is someone who has the desire for this type of self discipline. This type of self discipline isn't a denial of oneself but a full achievement of self actualization.

Drugs and Psychic Ability:

There are some people who believe that taking drugs can increase psychic ability, but that's not really the case. Under the right conditions, drugs like marijuana or psilocybin can cause a type of shamanic experience that does involve psychic insights. This happens because most people have been conditioned by society to not use their psychic abilities, and when someone takes a psychedelic drug it can temporarily break this social conditioning; in such a case the drug experience might let psychic insights in. Nevertheless there are dangers associated with taking such drugs, and therefore this handbook does not recommend any drug use for psychic development. Furthermore, it needs to be pointed out that, in the long run, all drugs and alcohol decrease psychic ability.

It isn't just recreational drugs which decrease psychic ability, medical and psychiatric drugs often diminish psychic ability as well. Sometimes for health reasons a person may need to take medical drugs, and this handbook isn't encouraging anyone to stop taking necessary medical drugs. However, there are many experts who have publicly stated that psychiatric drugs are being over-prescribed at this time in our society. Nevertheless withdrawal from psychiatric drugs is only safely done with medical supervision; and personally I have known people who feel that they need psychiatric drugs to survive. So this handbook isn't encouraging you to do anything which would place you at risk. And we aren't giving medical or psychiatric advice. But it has to be pointed out that the chronic use of drugs does suppress psychic development and may prevent the full emergence of psychic abilities. Therefore it should be mentioned that sometimes there are legitimate holistic health alternatives to taking medical drugs; this may be something you may wish to research. In developing psychic abilities, the dedicated student should avoid drugs whenever it's safe and healthy to do so. In a society where so many people become dependent upon drugs and alcohol, it's no wonder that so many people deny the possibility of psychic power.

Drugs and alcohol can be used to stimulate endorphins which create pleasure, but there are better ways of doing that. Endorphins can be stimulated through healthy exercise and other activities like yoga or exercise. Creating positive social experiences can stimulate endorphins. Even simple breathing exercises, when done correctly can stimulate endorphins.

Evoking the Spirit from Within

The Latin root word for "spirit" literally means breath or to breathe. Spirit is what animates life, and this animation is visibly seen in the act of breathing. This insight is relevant in understanding the training practice for this lesson.

Training Practice

In all forms of meditation the ego can be a problem if it asserts itself continually into the consciousness of the meditator. In ordinary life, you do need an ego, but in meditation you don't. So that if you can set your ego aside for a while, that would be good.

But another aspect of ego is that it can be healed by meditation. Meditation can sometimes help the ego to redefine itself, making it more positive.

Another point worth mentioning is that an invocation need not be elaborate. A simple phrase like, "I love life." can invoke the spirit of life. If combined with breathing exercises, this can bring forth life's energies.

Breathing exercises when done correctly can be a spiritual experience. There are many spiritual disciplines which make use of breathing exercises. Yoga is one example. However for our purposes of developing psychic abilities, this breathing exercise should take a certain form. Again we will use the psychic scanning technique with its pattern of scan/subvocalize/cognize.

SCAN: In this case, you will scan your lungs through the act of breathing. When you inhale or exhale, you are making a perception of your lungs. This is literally true. Your physical body, through your nervous system, has internal perceptions. If, for example, you were hungry, you would feel the hunger inside of your stomach. But not all internal physical perceptions are unpleasant, some are pleasant and some are neutral. So by the same token, you can feel your lungs when you breathe in or out. To scan something is to place your conscious awareness upon something. In psychic scanning you are often extending your feelings to outside of your body; before you can learn to do that, you must be able to focus upon the feelings you have inside of your body. When you breathe in, you will be scanning your lungs by feeling your lungs expand. When you breathe out, you will be scanning your lungs by feeling your lungs contract.

For this exercise it's best if you sit comfortably in a chair that has a straight back. Make sure to maintain good posture. Breathe from your chest at your heart level. If you can do this comfortably, breathe in by pushing out your chest thus causing your lungs to expand. Reverse the process when you exhale by contracting your chest as you exhale from your upper lungs.

Try this:
Purse your lips slightly and breathe out through your mouth, then breath in through your nose. But always breathe in what way feels most natural for you. Always make sure you get enough air and avoid hyperventilating.

As a prerequisite to the full drill, practice this slow deep breathing from the chest until you can do it habitually without having to really think about it. As you breathe, do it in a way that is comfortable to you. If you can breathe in deeply that's good, if it's comfortable. But comfort is the key. Don't push yourself past your comfort zone. Never push yourself past the point of safety. Breathe in as deeply as you can and breathe out as completely as you can. Breathe in and out as slowly and deliberately as you can. Don't allow yourself to hyperventilate. Be sensitive to your feelings as you breathe.

Scan your lungs by paying attention to your feelings in your lungs. Practice this type of deep breathing until you find a comfortable pattern and the practice becomes automatic.

SUBVOCALIZE: After every breath in and out, you will then briefly subvocalize after you exhale. What you will subvocalize is a short affirmation that expresses your gratitude for your life. Make this affirmation as simple as possible. Keep this affirmation short.

We suggest, "I love life."

Whatever affirmation you use, it should be a positive expression of your love of life.

COGNIZE: After you subvocalize, you will momentarily close your eyes and pay attention to your feeling of gratitude for life. This gentle closing and opening of your eyes should take about three seconds.

During this momentary closing of your eyes you may see a brief visual image or you may not. But don't force yourself to imagine anything. However, you are inviting images or feelings to enter your mind based on your love of life.

So after you subvocalize the affirmation of gratitude for your life, you may *feel* your connection to all life. It is through this feeling, that you *know* that you are connected to all living things though the life force generated by the Earth's ecosystem. Of course, your physical body is a part of the Earth's ecosystem. Therefore this cognition is your awareness of your emotional connection with all life in the ecosystem.

Simply focus upon feeling a love for life. It's important that you feel your love for life so that you know your love for life. In this case, you know by feeling. As you focus in on this knowingness, close your eyes momentarily so as to turn your attention inward, then immediately open your eyes.

Repeat the Pattern: So in this breathing practice you have a repeated three-part pattern. You first scan your lungs as you breathe in and out. Secondly you subvocalize a brief affirmation of love for life. And thirdly you center your awareness by momentarily closing your eyes in a spiritual knowingness and then opening them. This brief spiritual knowingness is your cognition.

A *cognition* may be thought of in terms of a unit of time. This closing and opening of your eyes is a three second unit of time. In this system of psychic practice we call this a cognate. In this handbook, the term "cognate" is given a specialized meaning.

So here is our unique definition of the word. The Latin root words for cognate means *together with*. A cognate is a single unit which *together with* other cognates makes up a longer cognition. This unit of time is so short that it's really only about three seconds. A single cognate could take place in the time it takes you to close and open your eyes. So what you are doing in this particular drill is to invite into your consciousness a single cognate. You don't have to blink your eyes to have a cognition, but in this drill, that is the mechanism used. Other training practices in this book use other physical mechanisms to invite cognition. The time of a longer cognition would be made up of many short units of time. So a cognition is made up of many units of cognates.

When you use scan/subvocalize/cognize in candle gazing you might have had long periods of cognition. Such a cognition would be made up of hundreds of cognates. But for the purpose of this breathing drill, you want the cognition to be as brief as possible; that would be a single cognate, the time it takes to intentionally close and open your eyes.

So this is how you apply the pattern of scan/subvocalize/cognize to your breathing exercise in six exact steps:

1. Sit down in a comfortable chair.

2. Start the cycle of this exercise by breathing in and then exhaling.

3. Briefly subvocalize a short affirmation such as, "I love life."

4. Gently close and open your eyes to experience a single cognate.

5. Continue with this cycle scan/subvocalize/cognize for as long as you feel comfortable in doing so.

6. End the cycle by returning your breathing to normal; then stretch your arms and make sure that you haven't become lightheaded from hyperventilating before you stand up.

This cycle of scan/subvocalize/cognize is done over and over so that your act of breathing becomes an ongoing affirmation of gratitude for life. This practice of breath control can be done for as long as you feel good doing it.

This has the potential to be exhilarating. At first it will just be a hassle as you concentrate upon mastering the process. But when the process becomes automatic and habitual, you will find that your cognate contains the feeling of bliss. Every time you close and open your eyes you will have a brief moment of spiritual joy. You may see a brief visual image when you close your eyes. But don't worry about whether you do or don't see an image in your mind's eye. When practiced enough times, this breathing exercise becomes an ecstasy producing process. This is because you are using your own bioenergy to directly stimulate the endorphin producing function of your brain. With practice this will come about automatically. The ecstasy you will feel from doing this will produce greater joy than taking drugs or any other addictive habits.

As a practice, this serves several purposes. One thing is that it is another step in developing an effective psychic scanning technique. It also evokes awareness of the body's natural life force. Furthermore, it enhances self discipline. In order to fully develop psychic ability some students may have to quit or reduce alcohol consumption, or that of some other substance. This breathing exercise can help with that because in this practice the student is asserting the predominance of the spiritual body over the physical body.

You should try this technique over a period of days. Give yourself a good chance to see how it works for you.

Practice Swings

However, it's possible that this particular technique of meditation doesn't bring you to bliss. But even if it doesn't result in bliss, this training practice will help you to learn how to use the scan/subvocalize/cognize method.

This scan/subvocalize/cognize method can also be called *psychic scanning*. Although you are not using your psychic powers in this breathing exercise, you are practicing with the techniques of scan, subvocalize and cognize. If you were training yourself to play baseball, you might start off with *practice swings* of the bat, that is, you would practice swinging the bat correctly before you attempted to hit a baseball. By using a structured breathing exercise to work with these scan, subvocalize, cognize methods, you are preparing yourself to use psychic scanning.

This method has many potential psychic applications, even some not described in this book. These applications of psychic scanning may be discovered by you on your own after you've passed through the psychic threshold. Once you've learned psychic scanning through structured training practices, there's no limits to what you can do with it.

Find Your Bliss-Creating Meditation Technique

But first you do need to find a technique of meditation which brings you to bliss. The candle gazing technique from the previous lesson might be useful. Some people need a meditative *physical activity* like walking or working in a garden. There are other techniques, described in this book which can be useful. Different meditation methods work for different individuals. Whatever meditative practice gives you peace of mind and brings you to bliss is what you should use. Some people use drugs or alcohol to relax, but that's really a mistake because you pay too high a price for your relaxation. You need something that leaves you clear minded afterwards. For some people, sitting and listening to relaxing music may do this. Consider what activity is healthful, harmless, relaxes you and makes you feel good. That's your bliss-creating meditation technique. Such meditation is a necessary tool for survival in this world.

A drug addict, for example, has lost control over his life and physical body; this is because the addiction has dominated his physical body to the point where will power and reason have become meaningless. When a meditation technique is mastered, the spiritual body is reasserting dominance over the physical body, if only for a short period of time. With the continuing practice of meditation, the addict will come to realize that his or her will power can be utilized to take back control away from the addiction. Of course, withdrawal from drug addiction, in order to be safe, may require medical supervision.

The Benefits of Breath Meditation

But do try to learn the meditation method of this breathing exercise because it reinforces the pattern of scan/subvocalize/cognize which has many other applications in psychic ability. As well as that, it trains you in yet another way to enhance your ability to maintain mental concentration over longer periods of time. This concentration training is similar in purpose to that of the candle gazing practice.

Also this practice trains you in the habit of slow deep breathing, so that you will start to habitually breath in a healthy way. This habit of slow deep breathing increases your oxygen intake which in turn enhances physical and brain health. As you learn this method, you may find that your breathing becomes deeper and more complete. When you breathe deeply, air enters your lower lungs as well as your upper lungs. You expand your lower lungs by pushing out with your diaphragm. Thus you take in more air with every breath. This is known to be good for heart health as well as brain function. The more times you practice this, the more that this healthy breathing will become habitual. And once it does becomes habitual, you'll do it automatically in other situations.

Before you go on to the next lesson, make sure that you have mastered this technique described above for a breathing exercise. You will know that you have mastered this technique when it becomes so practiced that it is automatic. During your psychic development training, try to periodically use this practice for at least ten minutes per meditation session.

If you have issues with addiction, consider using this or some other meditation practice for longer periods of time. Use meditation to lessen or eliminate your addiction. This is because you really won't have much success in reaching your full psychic potential if you are addicted to drugs or alcohol. For some people, moderate use of marijuana or alcohol may seem to enhance their lifestyle. That's for you to decide. The question you should ask is: Is this drug my servant or am I its slave?

. Lesson Fourteen .

The EEG machine is a device that measures brain waves. Hans Berger, the man who invented it, became a student of neuroscience because of a psychic experience that he had. Berger was nearly killed in an accident where a horse came close to running over him. The incident greatly startled him. He was surprise when, later, a telegram reached him from miles away. At the same instant that he was nearly killed, his sister had experienced a strong feeling of danger which she associated with him. She inquired after him out of concern. He realized that his sister had experienced a psychic insight. This changed the course of his life. He began studying the brain as a way of understanding psychic phenomena. Although he never developed a science for psychic ability, in more recent years, the study of brain activity has contributed to the development of psychic technology.

bioenergy: *noun,* this would be all forms of energy connected to life. Photosynthesis in plants, for example, would be an expression of bioenergy. The electrochemical functions of the brain and nervous system would be bioenergy. The digestive processes of the body involve bioenergy.

cognate: *noun,* in this handbook, this term is given a special, unique meaning. Cognition is realization or understanding, it is the mental acquisition of knowledge. A cognition is a realization. Think of a cognition as being built up of a set of smaller cognitions. The smallest unit of cognition is a cognate. A cognate takes place so fast that it happens in the time it takes to close and open your eyes. A single cognate may not be intellectually comprehended, it comes across more like a feeling. If knowledge can be thought of as a mental construction, a cognate is a single building block of that construction.

Gaian life force: *noun,* this would be the life energy created and utilized by the the Earth's ecosystem. This isn't exactly the same as Divine Source Energy, because Divine Source Energy is purely spiritual. But the Divine Source is ultimately the source of all things, and that includes the energies which make up the material universe. The Gaian life force is the collective intelligence and bioenergy of the biosphere of Earth. The Gaian life force is both bioenergy and the living intelligence of the Earth acting in unison to direct all life forms on Earth.

All of the living things on Earth are connected together by the Gaian life force. The bioenergy used by living things is influenced by both the laws of nature and the subtle influence of the planetary consciousness of the living Earth. The planet Earth isn't just a big rock floating in space, it is a living and intelligent being brought into being by the Divine Source.

Gaia is a name used in bioscience for the ecosystem when its actions are conceived of holistically. Gaia is also an ancient name for Mother Earth, or if you will, the Earth Goddess. The Gaian life force is therefore the living energy created by the ecosystem. You are a part of the ecosystem, therefore this living energy can be felt within you. For example, when you breathe, the Gaian life force is actively involved in the process.

However, there is a difference between the Divine Source Energy and the Gaian life force; the Divine Source Energy does only good and never causes harm, yet this isn't always true for the Gaian life force. The Gaian life force has three aspects: creativity, preservation and destruction. The Gaian life force inspires birth and survival, but it can also inspire the energy of violence; when one animal hunts and kills another animal that would be an energetic expression of the Gaian life force through natural instincts.

This is not to say that the Gaian life force is evil. You need the Gaian life force for as long as you physically live in the world, but you need to keep your personality centered in an awareness of the Divine Source Energy.

The Gaian life force is empowering, but it can become a channel for negative emotions such as fear or anger. Love is the only emotion associated with the Divine Source Energy. The Gaian life force can be an expression of a wide spectrum of emotions such as *fear, anger, disgust, aggression, contentment, sensuality,* or *happiness*. The trick to happiness isn't to suppress your negative emotions, but to center your awareness in love so that you don't become stuck in fear or anger. When you are fully feeling all of your emotions, you are fully connected to the Gaian life force.

Dynamics of Mind

The different dynamics of mind can be represented in the

different ways you breathe.

Consider this:

When you are asleep, your mind is unconscious and yet you breathe automatically. During your normal waking time you also tend to breathe automatically, until you place some of your attention upon your breathing, whereupon it becomes a conscious act. If you were involved in a sporting event, your primary attention would be upon the competition, but you might have to occasionally pay attention to your breathing as well, for example when you struggle to catch your breath; thus in that situation your breath control would be *semi-conscious* in that it would be habitual at times but also consciously controlled at times. But with training, you could condition the habitual functions of your mind so that you breathe in a better way, and this too would be a use of the semi-conscious mental function because it would involve the conscious intention to influence a normally unconscious process. So the process of breathing involves the mind's interaction between conscious and unconscious mental functions.

If you were looking at a horror movie where you were frightened by something that you saw, this might influence your subconscious mind to cause an involuntary change in the pattern of your breathing.

If you use breathing as a spiritual practice, you might come to feel periods in which you experience spiritual joy, and during such periods of spiritual joy, you would be aware of your superconscious mind which is the source of your spiritual intelligence.

Your mind arises from consciousness, and every aspect of mind represents an expression of consciousness. The mind is a complex system and has many different aspects depending upon how you analyze it; for the purposes of this handbook, there are five basic dynamics of mind that you need to understand. These are *conscious mind, subconscious mind, semiconscious mind, unconscious mind,* and *superconscious mind*.

subconscious mind: *noun,* the aspect of mind which develops in the infant prior to an understanding of language. This pre-lingual, non-linguistic aspect of mind functions perfectly well for the infant although it's not dependent upon spoken or written language. The word semantic refers to something that relates to language. The subconscious mind could also be called the non-semantic mind because it doesn't depend on language. Or it could be called the pre-semantic mind because it originally developed prior to the individual's apprehension of language.

The subconscious mind is the first mind of the individual, and it thinks without using language. The subconscious mind is intuitive, imaginative and feeling-based. The subconscious mind remains with the individual throughout life, but as the child learns more and more language, the childlike subconscious mind sinks below the level of consciousness.

As the child grows up, the adult mind learns to think more and more with language and becomes less aware of those mental functions which are non-linguistic. However, this subconscious mind asserts itself through the practice of art forms and through sleep dreams. Sensitivity to the subconscious mind can be a basis for intuitive awareness.

conscious mind: *noun,* this is the aspect of mind that you use when you are fully awake and aware of your present time surroundings. Although the conscious mind is not devoid of intuitive awareness, it is founded primarily on language. It is the adult, mature mind. The conscious mind is logical and centers itself in physical awareness. The conscious mind expresses itself through the physical body, but it can also be aware of spiritual influences.

semi-conscious mind: *noun,* this is the mind that both develops new habitual behaviors and directs these habitual behaviors once they have been learned. This is habitual mind is associated with certain centers in the brain, both in deep brain structures and the cortex.

The use of these habitual functions does not require full conscious awareness. For example, you learned to develop the habit of walking when you were a child. Walking involves complex muscles movements and physical balancing, but as an adult you probably take the complexity of this physical action for granted because it now takes very little conscious attention to walk. When you are talking with someone as you walk along, your conscious attention would be on the conversation, not the act of walking. Walking has likely become for you a semi-conscious function. However it's partially conscious because you do make conscious decisions relating to it. You consciously decide when to walk, how fast you will walk and things of that sort. But as an adult, you typically take for granted the complex muscle movements necessary for walking because they have become so automatic. So walking is a semi-conscious function.

Any routine behavior, through training, can go from being

conscious to semi-conscious. If you were to learn to ride a bicycle, for example, at first it would require all of your concentration to pedal, balance and steer. Eventually your habitual mind will respond to all of your conscious training so that the newly conditioned habits become semi-conscious. So that with training you learn to ride the bicycle without full conscious concentration.

Development of the semiconscious mind is significant in meditation training. At first meditation training requires a conscious and focused concentration. With training the meditation practices become habitual, just like walking.

unconscious mind: *noun,* these are the functions of the brain which take place automatically without any conscious supervision. Basically this is the *autonomic nervous system*. However, within the nomenclature of this handbook, this isn't to be confused with the subconscious mind.

It should be pointed out that as a living thing, the physical body has its own consciousness which is the consciousness of the Gaian life force. When the physical body dies, the spiritual body permanently leaves it immediately. The spiritual body operates the physical body through the brain, and when brain-death happens, the spiritual connection to the physical vehicle is terminated. However, it takes some time for all the cells to die. Hair cells may continue to grow for a time after death, for example. The spirit immediately leaves the body at death, but the Gaian life force slowly retreats.

The spiritual body bonds, in a dedicated way, to its physical body at birth. Death occurs when the spiritual body chooses to permanently separate from the physical body, or when massive physical trauma occurs, forcing the spiritual body's permanent departure.

The unconscious mind does not rely on the consciousness coming from the soul, that's why in this handbook it's called unconscious instead of subconscious; but the unconscious mind does have its own type of consciousness which comes from the Gaian life force.

As a living human being your overall consciousness is a lifelong marriage between the Gaian life force channelled through your physical body and the pure Divine Source Energy channelled through your spiritual body.

superconscious mind: *noun*, this is the spiritual aspect of mind that is purely emergent from the psyche. This is the mind of your spiritual body. It is your soul-mind. This is the source of your greatest psychic abilities. This aspect of mind is incorporeal in that it isn't dependent upon the brain. And the superconscious mind is interfaced with the Spiritual Realm, so it is not responsive to self-centeredness or egotism.

The superconscious mind may, under certain conditions, interact with the brain. The superconscious mind does often emerge into brain activities through the subconscious mind. Much of the training described in this handbook teaches you how to allow your superconscious mind to interact with the other dynamics of mind.

All of these different dynamics of mind are interconnected, and the superconscious mind can interface with any other aspect of mind. As I have mentioned, the superconscious mind can influence the brain, but it also operates on its own, independent of the brain.

The superconscious mind is the mind created by your soul. The superconscious mind has the ability to recall all experiences from all of your previous incarnations, assuming that this isn't your first Earthly incarnation.

In deep meditation, when the act of meditating becomes habitual through training, the superconscious mind becomes more prevalent in your awareness. The knowledge which arises directly from the Spiritual Realm is manifested through the superconscious mind. The superconscious mind has the power to direct the Divine Source Energy.

For the living individual, there are always two mental systems; there is the mental system which arises from the Divine Source Energy and the mental system which arises from the Gaian life force. The Gaian life force is completely emergent in the unconscious mind. The Divine Source Energy is completely emergent in the superconscious mind.

Your awareness of both the Divine Source Energy and the Gaian life force is essential to your psychic development.

The subconscious mind can be conditioned so that it becomes a link between the conscious mind and the superconscious mind. And this is the essence of psychic training. What links the conscious mind and the subconscious mind together is the physical body. So the conscious mind receives information from the subconscious mind through a sensitivity to physical sensations. The conscious mind can send messages to the subconscious mind through visualizations, physical actions or a combination of visualization with physical action.

As an living Earthling, the interplay of the Divine Source Energy with the Gaian life force is a lifelong synergetic relationship. Likewise, the creative aspect of the living Earth is expressed through a synergetic relationship between the Earth's ecosystem and the Spiritual Realm. The beauty of the natural world is a reflection of the aesthetic essence of the Spiritual Realm. As a spiritual being operating a physical body on Earth, you are in the heart of this creative synergy.

The Gaian life force is the fusion of bioenergy with the intelligence of the Spiritual Realm. What might be described as mental waveforms arise from the Spiritual Realm. These mental waveforms connect with tangible forms of bioenergy. It's their complementary relationship which makes human life possible, as well as making all life on Earth possible.

The complexity of the human mind and the energies which make up life can't be comprehended fully with pure logic. Ultimately you must learn to apprehend this information intuitively. The intellect will only take you so far in your journey to awaken your psychic powers. At some point you will spontaneously transcend the intellect to directly cognize the nature of things. But this intellectual struggle, which takes place through study, helps to awaken your power of **intuitive cognition**.

Intuitive Cognition takes place when you open yourself to a free flowing stream of cognates. This is an indication that you are passing through a psychic threshold. Again, this is something you have to experience in order to understand it.

In the course of psychic training, the student is lead up to the point of reaching a psychic threshold. In fact, there may be a series of psychic thresholds. What will happen is that the student will begin to apprehend reliable knowledge directly through intuitive processes. This is not to say that the psychic practitioner abandons the processes of logic or sensory observation. But as intuition develops, the processes of logic and sensory observation are enhanced by what might be called *intuitive cognition*.

You can't gain psychic abilities merely through an academic study of the phenomena. But some intellectual understanding of the mind is necessary to the achievement of reaching the psychic threshold point.

Human consciousness can be defined, to some extent, by what is known as brainwave states. An EEG machine measures the frequency of brainwaves. Scientists recognize four distinct brainwave states: *Beta*, *Alpha*, *Theta* and *Delta*.

Beta waves are the fastest.

These brainwave states slow down progressively as they go from Beta to Alpha, then to Theta, then to Delta, which is the slowest.

These distinct brainwave states emerge under different conditions. Beta emerges when the individual is fully awake and active. Alpha emerges during periods of light relaxation. Theta emerges during periods of deep, trancelike relaxation. And Delta takes place in deepest sleep.

These four brainwave states describe four levels of conscious awareness. They describe the four levels of intensity with which the conscious mind is involved with directing the physical body. These four states go from full waking consciousness at the Beta state to full unconsciousness at the Delta state of deep sleep.

The dynamic relationship between incorporeal consciousness (which channels through the spiritual body) and corporeal consciousness (as expressed through the physical body) defines the focus of the conscious mind. Generally speaking, the more that the conscious mind is engaged in controlling the physical body, the more rapid become the brainwaves. The conscious mind is fully activated in the Beta state, but the conscious mind is deactivated in the Delta state.

An analogous way of thinking about this would be to consider the relationship between a driver and his automobile.

(Beta) When the driver is in heavy traffic, he would be very focused on the act of driving, and perhaps because of this he would feel stressed out.

(Alpha) As the traffic thins out, the driver would become more relaxed and might even turn on the radio to listen to pleasant music.

(Theta) When driving slowly down a deserted country lane, he might daydream and only pay casual attention to the road.

(Delta) And of course, when he comes home, parks the car and leaves it for a while, the driver has no consciousness of the car until he returns to it later on.

(Death and Reincarnation) When this car becomes too used-up and finally breaks down, then the driver gets rid of that car and finds a new one.

The psyche is the driver of the physical vehicle. It's through the focus of the conscious mind by which the psyche operates the physical body. The brainwave states of Beta, Alpha, Theta and Delta define the different degrees of intensity to which the conscious mind is engaged with the physical vehicle.

During sleep, the subconscious mind may express itself in profound ways. The subconscious mind may find an emotional outlet through sleep dreams. Because there's a great deal of emotional suppression in contemporary society, sometimes sleep dreams are the only way that the subconscious mind can express itself. Some artists draw inspiration from their sleep dreams as a way of expressing the subconscious mind through their art.

If a person begins to pay attention to his or her dreams, the ability of lucid dreaming may emerge spontaneously. This is where you are aware of the fact that you are dreaming when you are in a dream. This may allow you to control your dream in some way. Your dream-self may decide to fly or anything else that the imagination enacts within the dream world. Lucid dreaming takes place when the conscious mind is expressing itself to some degree through the dream environment created by the subconscious mind.

Persons who begin to pay attention to their dreams may find that they astral project spontaneously. The Astral Body is a mental projection of your physical body created by the superconscious mind. An Astral Body can operate during times when the spiritual body is out of the physical body. The Astral Body interfaces with the spiritual body when the spiritual body leaves the physical body during deep sleep.

Basically the Astral Body is the spiritual body; more accurately, you could say that the Astral Body is the conscious mind's awareness of the spiritual body when it journeys outside of the physical body.

During deep sleep, the spiritual body may leave the physical body for a time and wander around outside of it. Normally you have no conscious memory of this. This out-of-body experience isn't really dangerous. The unconscious mind automatically operates the physical body during these times of deep sleep. While the physical body is still alive, the spiritual body is attuned to the unique energetic signal of the brain and nervous system. Through a dedicated psychic connection, the spiritual body is always linked to the living physical body. Therefore the spiritual body automatically returns home whenever the physical body needs to awaken.

However, the experiences of the spiritual body aren't recorded as memories by the brain during these out-of-body ventures. When you awaken, the conscious mind, which is dependent upon brain-based memory, doesn't normally remember the out-of-body experience.

Nevertheless, the superconscious mind can create a mental projection of the physical body which becomes a configuration which is imposed upon the spiritual body. This intentional mental projection turns the spiritual body into an Astral Body during out-of-body experiences. This Astral Body is like a recording device which keeps a record of the perceptions of the spiritual body during these out-of-body experiences.

The spiritual body perceives reality differently than the physical body. So the Astral Body has to be able to translate spiritual perceptions into representations which can be interpreted as if they were sensory perceptions. The astral travel experiences have to be mentally translated from one type of perception to another. The Astral Body is designed by the superconscious mind so that it can mimic the physical body. Because of this, the Astral Body is able to create mental representations of the events experienced by the free-floating spiritual body. This Astral Body will remember these experiences upon returning to the physical body. As the Astral Body reintegrates with the physical body, those memories of astral projection are downloaded into the brain as neural memories. In this way the experience of astral projection may be remembered after awakening.

During lucid dreams or astral projection, the psychic talents possessed by the superconscious mind may be fully realized. Some psychics have precognitive dreams which they may remember when they awaken.

Through astral projection, some psychics observe remote locations and remember what they have observed when they return to normal consciousness. Psychics with advanced training in deep meditation are more likely to be able to astral project at will or to experience lucid dreaming. But astral projection techniques and lucid dreaming are not a part of this course; they are mentioned here because sometimes a psychic novice during training may spontaneously experience some of these things.

Although you may be a psychic novice in this incarnation, in a previous incarnation you may have had advanced psychic training. So these abilities, such as astral projection, may spontaneously emerge at any time in your training.

Astral projection or lucid dreaming may take place during the deep Theta state near Delta. This is the twilight region that hovers between deep sleep and drowsiness.

Meditation techniques create the conditions in which the brain of the practitioner goes into the Alpha state or the Theta state. The Alpha state of light relaxation and the Theta state of deep relaxation are ideal for meditation practice. As the conscious mind slows down during meditation, the natural healing functions of the autonomic nervous system can emerge to restore physical health. So it's optimal during the day to spend some time in the relaxing states of Alpha and Theta. This is why the regular practice of meditation is good for health.

The psychic Edgar Cayce once noted that the subconscious mind is the door to the superconscious mind.

The superconscious mind is the source of your psychic abilities; it is superconscious in that it transcends ordinary consciousness. Your superconscious mind is the non-corporeal aspect of the mind which is immortal. This is the aspect of mind which has stayed with your immortal spiritual body incarnation after incarnation. The subconscious mind operates on the basis of feeling and imagination, and these are necessary to comprehending the superconscious mind.

So to put this into simple words: you best access your

psychic abilities by using your emotional sensitivity and your imagination. You receive psychic knowledge with your emotional sensitivity and you project psychic energy with your imagination. But imagination can pollute the reception of psychic information. So be clear in your mind when your are using your imagination and when you are using your emotional sensitivity. When you close your eyes you invite imagination. So it's best to have your eyes open when you are being psychically receptive. And it's best to have your eyes closed when you are projecting psychic energy.

The conscious mind thinks in terms of language, but language-based thinking is dependent upon neurological functions. When the brain dies, language understanding dies with it. The superconscious mind has its own spiritual language which does not arise from the brain's language functions. The superconscious mind can use the imaginative, intuitive subconscious mind to translate this spiritual language into the neural-based language used by the conscious mind.

This is why the *psychic scanning* method of scan/subvocalize/cognize works. When you scan, you are being intuitive and imaginative. When you subvocalize you are being logical. When you intentionally engage the interplay of intuition and logic you stimulate cognition. Cognitive realization arises from the synchrony of the conscious and subconscious mind-dynamics.

All of this brings us to the relationship between the brain and the mind. Again, this handbook has its own way of defining these terms. The brain is the physical aspect of the mind. The brain operates on electrochemical functions.

The *mind* is often thought of as the functions of the brain as opposed to the material aspects of the brain. But really there is a corporeal mind and an incorporeal mind. The corporeal mind builds itself on the foundations created by the Gaian life force. The corporeal mind is the cellular matter, electrochemical energies and functions of the brain; the incorporeal mind is the consciousness and subatomic forces which are associated with the spiritual body.

The point of defining all of these terms is to discern the varying ways in which consciousness relates to the mind. The mind is the primary tool of the psychic practitioner. Consciousness is the foundation of the human mind and the Spiritual Realm. Archaic scientific thinking, which was based on the mechanical model of the universe, only attributed consciousness as a peculiar function of the human brain. But human consciousness through the brain is only one emergent manifestation of the underlying consciousness which permeates the entire material universe. Consciousness is the ultimate foundation for everything in the cosmos.

The mind of a human being is designed to operate on the interaction of logic with intuition. The old mechanical model of the universe was a concept based on one type of logical construction. Then, quantum physics came along with a different type of logical construction which could explain some things that the old mechanical model could not. Quantum physics opened the door to the realization that consciousness is the foundation of the cosmos. However, all scientific models of reality, quantum or otherwise, are based on logic. To really use your brain effectively you can't get stuck in logic, you must move back and forth between logic and intuition.

For example, in order to understand the meaning of this lesson that you are now reading, you must at times transcend your logic and use your intuitive understanding. These lessons are written in a way to force you to go back and forth between logic and intuition in order for you to understand them. The function of these lessons isn't so much to indoctrinate you with a philosophy as it is to awaken the necessary interplay of logic and intuition which leads to natural cognition. The lessons of this course are not found in these written words so much as they are found in your own self-realized cognitions.

The purpose of this particular lesson is to begin to familiarize you with the ideas that you will be using if you choose to actualize the more advanced expressions of psychic ability. Also this type of analysis is an intellectual exercise in identifying the complex ways in which consciousness relates to thought. But the only truth to be found in this lesson is your own self-realized truth.

Training Practice

The learning exercise for this lesson is to begin the practice of dream-recall journal writing. What is being suggested here is that you start keeping a type of journal in which you record your sleep dreams. It may not be possible for you to do this every morning, but if you leave a notebook and pen near your bed, you might find that you can do this on a regular basis. It's suggested that you keep doing this type of journal writing for as long as you are pursuing the development of your psychic powers.

This type of journaling is easy. When you wake up in the morning, write down in simple words a description of what you can recall of your sleep dreams.

Don't analyze these dreams for meaning. And don't worry about dream symbolism. In plain language just describe what you remember.

However, it's interesting to note that the Christian Bible does reference dream analysis several times. The prophets Joseph and Daniel could interpret dreams. And Christ's disciple Peter on at least one occasion interpreted a dream of his, and this dream helped to guide him in his leadership of the early Christian movement.

As you are training yourself in psychic development you might occasionally make reference to your own personal dream journal. From time to time, read what you've written in the journal and consider how it speaks to your feelings.

If you prefer, you can verbally record the dreams with an audio recorder rather than writing them down in a notebook. It's the act of describing your dreams in words that matters. This practice is an conscious observation of your subconscious mind. It's a way of creating a stronger link between your non-semantic subconscious mind and your semantic-based conscious mind. *Such a link is necessary in your psychic development because it can lead to the ability of spontaneous intuitive cognition.*

If you can do this type of dream journaling on a daily basis, that's good, but that may not be practical. So just do the dream journaling as often as you reasonably can. Use your intuition to determine how long you feel you need to maintain this practice. You might do this for a just a few weeks or you might use this practice for years.

It may happen that as you begin to pay attention to your dreams on a regular basis, you'll find that you spontaneously began to have lucid dreams or you may even find that you astral project at times. That isn't the purpose of the drill, but there's nothing wrong if this happens. Both lucid dreaming and astral projection are natural. However, sometimes people may become alarmed when they find themselves astral projecting for the first time. It can feel disturbing to see your physical body lying on the bed while you're looking down at it. Your Astral Body will function just as your physical body functions, but it will also respond to your intentions and thoughts. If you feel uncomfortable while you are outside of your physical body, just think the thought that you should return to it and make an intentional decision to do so. Once you are near your physical body, you can simply lie down into it and you will reintegrate and wake up.

. Lesson Fifteen .

When I was thirty years old, decades ago, I had a dream in which I felt that I left my body. In my dream, I rose up out of my body, and I flew up into the heavens. My perception of reality seemed heightened in my out-of-body experience. Colors were brighter, solid objects seemed more solid. I eventually found myself on the moon. On the surface was a table with a bizarre looking chess board. Playing a game of chess was Jesus Christ and Satan. If you can imagine a black hole in the shape of a human being, that's what Satan looked like. I felt terrified, as if my very soul was being judged. Eventually Jesus took a piece off of the chess board. He showed it to me. It was a little statue of me. He placed it in a box that looked like a Church and then smiled at me with compassion. My terror disappeared and I felt overwhelmed by love. I found myself flying back down to Earth again. Finally I returned to my physical body. I woke up, my heart beating furiously. My out-of-body experience had seemed more real to me than the world I had just woken up in.

Astral Body: *noun*, this is basically your spiritual body. However, it's your spiritual body when it's exterior to your still-living physical body. This is something you may experience when your physical body is asleep or unconscious. Normally your conscious mind resides in your physical body. Through training and strong intention you can learn to project your conscious mind into your Astral Body while you are in an out-of-body state. That is known as astral projection. To be able to astral project at will is an advanced skill. But sometimes novices will find that they spontaneously astral project during sleep. The word "astral" comes from a root word which means star. In ancient times, astronomers studied the stars not with telescopes but through natural astral projection. Your Astral Body is able to travel in space if you choose this. But this should not be the goal of a novice. And really astral projection serves no practical function. You can more easily practice remote viewing while safely occupying your physical body.

Non-Locality and Psychic Shield:

I am going to repeat some ideas that were already expressed because these ideas are important.

This lesson does have certain political implications in this limited sense. The oppressive globalist plutocracy known as the New World Order is headed by occultists. The real leaders of the world hide in the shadows and manipulate the publicly-known world leaders as if they were puppets. These plutocratic occultists use psychic power to remotely influence key persons in governments and corporations. Also some of these secret societies of occult practitioners use their knowledge of psychic power to attack their political enemies. If you've been opposing the New World Order, you may have been under psychic attack without realizing it. With what you will learn in this book and its training practices you will be able to become a psychic defender. You can use your psychic powers to shield yourself from attack or to shield other persons from attack. You can shield world leaders from demonic influence. There is a psychic war taking place on this planet. But being a psychic defender is never about projecting hatred to anyone. It's important to remember that all members of humanity are interconnected.

Until you understand the nature of the cosmos, you can't understand the significance of psychic ability. The true nature of the cosmos is that of interconnection. You see this interconnection manifesting itself in many different ways. A concept that describes one aspect of this interconnection is known as quantum non-locality.

Quantum non-locality is a proven principle of physics. This handbook isn't concerned with teaching physics, but you should know that everything in this system of psychic training is in harmony with advanced understandings of science. Quantum non-locality may refer to two quantum particles that are entangled. The behavior of these two particles is connected even when they're far apart; this is because they have a non-local connection. This means that it is not the energy and matter in the intervening space that connects them. At a foundational level of the material universe is an *information field*. This information field is the Spiritual Realm. Everything is interconnected through the Spiritual Realm.

Another concept related to non-locality is synchronicity. Synchronicity takes place where there is an observable relationship between two events which are not connected through the normal mechanism of cause and effect. A cause and effect relationship is what we usually see in the material universe. If you hit a billiard ball across the table into another billiard ball causing it to move, that would be a cause and effect relationship. However, a non-local connection doesn't need for one object to move through space to another object. It would be as if you wiggled a billiard ball on one side of the table and that in turn caused a billiard ball on the other side of the table to wiggle. This isn't how things normally work in the world we can observe with our sensory perceptions, however, through the invisible Spiritual Realm, all things are connected. Synchronicity can explain why astrology can be used to explain the influence of distant planetary bodies upon human affairs.

Non-local connections can be observed between human beings. When a mother bonds with her infant, even when she is apart from her child, she can feel what's happening with her baby. If people pray for someone who is ill, they will tangibly assist the patient with his or her healing process. The remote viewing of distant environments has been proven by scientists. Reiki and other holistic healing methods use remote healing techniques. Non-locality is the basis of psychic abilities.

There have been controlled studies which show that if a person is prayed for by others, even if he doesn't know that he's being prayed for, that person will recover faster than a person with the exact same ailment who isn't prayed for. This is the basis of Reiki remote healing. Reiki healing practice gives a precise structure to the prayer process which makes it very effective. But Reiki practice has no monopoly on remote healing. If you say a prayer with strong intention for the Divine Source Energy to heal yourself or someone else, the Divine Source will send the Divine Source Energy to you or another. You may or may not find it useful to learn Reiki practice from a Reiki master. But whether or not you study Reiki, you can easily perform remote healing through simple prayer. Once you have established your positive relationship with the Divine Source, all you have to do is to evoke your awareness of the Divine Source Energy and intend for the Divine Source Energy to be sent to whomever you choose, and it will be done.

Sometimes theological arguments get in the way of this simple process. For example, I once heard a person say that since God is all knowing and all loving, it didn't matter if you pray because God knows who needs help and provides such help automatically. I would contend that there is a reason why you do have to go to all the bother of praying. This is because God grants us free will. You must choose of your own free will to invoke the Holy Spirit which comes from God. This healing energy is directed by your soul's desires, and it responds to mental intentions. Although it's freely available to all, you must choose to invoke it, God will not force it upon you.

The Divine Source Energy does only good and can do no harm, but that isn't the case for the Gaian life force. Nevertheless, the Gaian life force can be directed for the purpose of healing. For example, if you give another person a therapeutic massage, that will evoke the healing aspect of the Gaian life force. If you give another person a friendly hug, that will evoke the Gaian life force to heal yourself and the other person. These things evoke the preserving and healing aspect of the Gaian life force. Furthermore, the Gaian life force may work more quickly than the subtle influence of the Divine Source Energy.

The Gaian life force can evoke creative energy. Sex is an expression of the creative aspect of the Gaian life force.

But the Gaian life force can also be destructive. When two men get in a fist fight, they are expressing the destructive aspect of the Gaian life force.

The Gaian life force can be *healing/preserving, creative/ sexual* or *destructive/violent*.

Sometimes occult dabblers use the Gaian life force to express the lower vibrational energies of psychic power. This is an unethical use of psychic power. Using the healing and preserving aspect of Gaian life force can be effective in the healing process. But some occult dabblers try to combine sexual practices to evoke psychic powers. This is sometimes called sex magick. The letter "k" is added to indicate that this isn't stage magic. Although some occultists do get the results they want from this, it is nonetheless unethical. Lovemaking is a beautiful act between consenting adults, but occultists prostitute these sexual energies when they use them for the psychic manipulation of others. Also, at this time in this world, some extremely unethical occultists use animal sacrifice and even human sacrifice to evoke psychic powers. This is an abuse of the Gaian life force. Some occultists use their mental powers to take advantage of the principle of non-locality in unethical ways. An unethical occultist might direct psychic energies to confuse the mind of another person or even to make that person ill. In our contemporary world, there are secret societies which teach their members such techniques. And some of the most powerful people in the world are members of those secret societies.

This is why the tactic of psychic shielding is important to psychic development. In order to create a psychic shield you need to do three things:

1. Center yourself in an awareness of love for the Divine Source.
2. Affirm an attitude of good will for yourself and all humanity.
3. Affirm and visualize yourself and those you most care about as being surrounded by an aura of glowing light.

By doing these things repeatedly, you develop a habitual use of psychic ability which protects you automatically from negative non-local psychic connections and attracts positive non-local psychic connections. This is the art and science of psychic self defense.

There are also some things which tend to open you to psychic attack. Occult dabbling is dangerous because it may open you to psychic influences for which you aren't ready. Often people experiment with psychic techniques without realizing that they can open themselves to negative influences. Drug addiction and alcohol abuse can weaken your natural psychic shield. Even legally prescribed medical and psychiatric drugs can weaken your natural psychic shield. Of course, if you're using drugs for recreational purposes you have the option to quit, however this may not be the case with medicines. Nevertheless, anything you can do to minimize your drug use without harming your health is important. Compulsive negative attitudes can open you to negative psychic influences. It's best if you don't obsess on hatred, desire for revenge or irrational fears. Good general health practices can help you to maintain your natural psychic shield. Spend time in the sunshine when you can. If you can, it's best to eat a healthy diet, sleep well and exercise appropriately. When you center your awareness on a love for the Divine Source and empathy for your fellow human beings, your psychic shield will naturally be strengthened by these positive attitudes.

Training Practice

Say a prayer for yourself or somebody else. If you ask the Divine Source to send the Divine Source Energy to heal yourself or another, the Divine Source will do this. First you evoke your awareness of the Divine Source Energy. You may do this by sincerely saying a simple prayer or affirmation. Then you formally ask the Divine Source to send the Divine Source Energy to yourself or another person for the purpose of healing. It's your strong intention which makes this work.

However, the more ritualistically you do this the better. You can word this type of prayer in any way that makes sense to you, and you can develop rituals in any way that feels good to you. But complex rituals aren't necessary. You might do something like read something from a book of spiritual wisdom before praying then after praying touch your heart center and then your forehead. If you do something like that before and after saying a simple prayer it can be very effective.

This is one way you might say a healing prayer. Bow your

head, close your eyes, and place the palms of your hands together. First say something like this:

> *Beloved Divine Source, I am very grateful for all the health you have allowed my loved ones and me. Thank you for the many blessings you've given us. Thank you for your grace. You are the one true source of creation and I worship only you. Please send the Divine Source Energy to assist in my healing and the healing of (state that person's name). I am open to your healing power. I am open to your wisdom. Truly.*

After you've said the prayer, maintain the attitude of reverence for a while. Close your eyes and visualize yourself and the person you've prayed for as being healthy and fully recovered.

You can support your visualization process with subvocalization. For example you might subvocalize,

> *I see myself and (state person's name) fully healed and healthy.*

Simple prayer is easy, and it's a good starting point for training. While you are in training to develop psychic ability, frequently say simple prayers for yourself or others.

Specifically say healing prayers with great frequency. Think of people you know, (you don't even have to be close to them) and say prayers for those persons. If you hear about strangers with health problems in the news or from gossip, say prayers for them. If you hear of a person who is ill, say a prayer for that person. Pray for the homeless persons who you have seen during the day. All these prayers are to be said when you are in a remote location from the person or persons you are praying for.

It's perfectly acceptable to say prayers for yourself as well.

During the period when you are in psychic training, take some time on a regular basis and say prayers. The more you do this, the easier it will become for you to consciously direct the Divine Source Energy at will. This is your rightful inheritance as a child of the Divine Source.

. Lesson Sixteen .

Stand fast therefore in the liberty wherewith Christ hath made us free, and not be entangled again with the yoke of bondage ... For we through the Spirit hope for the righteousness by faith ... For the law is fulfilled in one word, even in this; Thou shall love they neighbor as thyself ... If we live in the Spirit let us also walk in the Spirit.

Galatians

Early Christianity

In the earliest days of Christianity, it was more of a spiritual movement rather than a formal religion. The Gospels (good news) were not written down, they were spoken stories about the life of Christ. Although the Gospels would eventually be written down, the religion was first spread by word of mouth. What Jesus taught was love: that you should love God, and love your neighbors as you love yourself. The followers of Jesus told stories of healing and miracles performed by Him. The Jews had been expecting the Messiah to come. Many Greeks and Romans anticipated the coming of a spiritual leader known as the Christ, the anointed one. The early followers believed that Jesus Christ was the son of God. Jesus had said that we are all the children of God. People believed that Jesus had died on the cross so that all who believe in

Him would be spiritually saved and their sins forgiven. It was a common practice before and during the time of Jesus that animal sacrifice be performed in atonement, so that God, or the gods, would forgive sins. The death of Jesus made such animal sacrifices unnecessary. The resurrection of Jesus gave hope of salvation after death.

In those early days of Christianity, there were severe punishments made by the Roman government for those who converted to Christianity, but becoming a Christian was fairly simple. You became a Christian by accepting Jesus Christ as the Messiah, only begotten son of God, and you witnessed to others that you believed in Jesus Christ. In those days, this was actually a crime, and you could be put to death for committing this crime. So the converts to Christianity had to be highly committed.

If you were a Christian you believed that Jesus was the son of God, of the same loving spiritual essence as God. You believed that you were a child of God. You believed in His teachings of love. You accepted His grace and lived a life of decency and gratitude. You faced your death with dignity knowing that your salvation was assured by your faith in God. And these early followers of Jesus Christ witnessed and experienced miracles.

In the early days of the Christian movement there were no complex doctrines to memorize, no dogmatic teachings that you had to swear by and no long list of strict rules that you were expected to obey without question. All these would come much later on as Christianity became a highly organized religion.

Religion is not always a good thing. With religious organization comes power, and power can be abused.

I'm not going to offer to recruit you into a Christian church. I'm not even a member of a Christian church at this time. I became a follower of Jesus Christ a little more than thirty years ago. I was baptized as a Christian a little more than fifteen years ago. I was a member of a Christian church for a year. I sometimes go to church on Saturday or Sunday. But I am not promoting the Church of Christianity. I am involved in a spiritual movement of Christians. But we are not like the modern church-going Christians, we are like the early Christians. We don't have dogma and doctrine and rules. The technology of psychic awakening has made all of that unnecessary, and once you pass through the major psychic thresholds, you don't need the technology. We who have awakened just have faith and miracles, as did the early Christians.

Secluded Prayer Groups

As it was for the early Christians, many members of this Christian movement of psychic Christians are hunted by members of certain branches of the government. I am a psychic Christian. My personal psychic powers are rather limited when compared to the other psychic Christians I have known. I don't hate the government or anything like that, but I am aware that certain government officials are sometimes obsessed with things that they can't control. Persons with powerful psychic abilities frighten some people in the government. So the powerful psychic Christians I've known choose to remain anonymous for the sake of their families and themselves.

They practice their psychic techniques in secluded prayer groups. They conceal their psychic powers from the general public. But they do use their psychic powers to heal people, to create prosperity for themselves and to subtlety influence the political system. I have seen these people perform miracles in the name of Jesus Christ.

Although I am not a powerful psychic, I do have an ability that is useful to this group. I can write and publish books. Also, importantly, I can't be traced back to any of the members of this group of psychic Christians. I have no family, social or business connections to them. They selected me as the outlet for this book of theirs mainly because their group's founder, James, did know me from experiences we shared when I was young. Also, some of them listened to a radio program that I was once on several years ago. In listening to what I had to say on the air, they decided that I was a kindred spirit, and so we began to meet in private. They would meet with me covertly, wearing disguises and withholding their real names. We would meet in secluded locations where they explained to me the information that would result in this book. After James died, Deborah became their leader and she met with me to create this final revised edition. So I am the author and publisher of this book, but I did not develop this system. Powerful Christian psychics did that. I merely describe their system.

The Body of Christ in the World

Christ came into the world taking the form of a human being, and in assuming the limitations of the flesh took the form of a specific person with a specific gender, racial identity and nationality. But the ascended Christ is of both genders, of all races and of all nationalities. For the ascended Christ has transcended the limits of flesh, but in a sense, Christ is still in the flesh in that He is now seen in His followers. We who believe in Christ and publicly affirm that belief make up the body of Christ in the world.

A choice is being offered to you now, before you continue your training to develop your psychic powers further. Nobody is asking you to join a Christian church. You can be a member of a Christian church or not. That is not relevant to your psychic development. In the Introduction to this book, I told you that you don't have to be a religious Christian in order to learn this system, and you don't. But, if you have not done so already, I am going to suggest that you consider becoming a follower of Jesus Christ. This would be useful if you are to continue your training in this system.

Prior to this lesson, you were encouraged to use a terminology that allowed you to somewhat ignore the fact that you were working with a system of Christian psychic training. Perhaps you have seen the development of your psychic powers. If so, perhaps you wish to continue with this development. If so, you have the opportunity to now accept the fact that you now have a spiritual relationship with Jesus Christ.

Why Accepting Christ is Difficult for Some

But I do understand why some persons resist accepting Jesus Christ. If that is the case for you, ask yourself these questions below. I suggest that you write down the answers to these questions as you go over them.

Do you recall a Christian who was a hypocrite, preaching one thing but living in another way? If so, who was it and what was the hypocrisy?

Do you recall a Christian or group of Christians who insulted you or hurt you in some way? What happened?

Was the Bible interpreted in some way for you that you found offensive or were in disagreement with? If so, what was this?

Do you feel that Christian teachings would restrict or limit you in some way that you could not accept? What would this be?

Did you ever know any Christians that you just didn't like or couldn't identify with? If so, what didn't you like about them?

Did you ever feel that you were unworthy to be a Christian or that Jesus Christ would never accept you? Why?

What you need to understand now is this

- Jesus Christ is perfect, but His followers in the world are not.

- The Kingdom of Jesus Christ in Heaven is perfect, but the Church of Jesus Christ in the world is not.

- The guidance which comes from Jesus Christ is perfect, but the teachings of Christian ministers in the world are not.

- There are many different Christian churches and movements in the world, but you don't have to like them all in order to be a follower of Jesus Christ.

- You don't have to be a perfect person in order to be accepted by Jesus Christ, you only have to believe in Him and open your heart to His guidance through the Holy Spirit.

If you have recently accepted Christ as your savior, I suggest that you pray to Him and ask for guidance to lead you to resources, persons or organizations that can help you in your walk with Christ.

If you did write down answers to the questions asked above, I suggest that you take the paper that you've written on and burn it in some safe way right now before reading more of this lesson.

Terminology for a New Era of Christianity

Divine Source = Our Father in Heaven
Anointed Savior = Jesus Christ
Divine Source Energy = Holy Spirit
Spiritual Realm = Heaven, or the Kingdom of God.
matrix of fear = satan, lucifer, the devil, all demons & hell

Accepting Jesus Christ as your Savior

1. Center yourself in feelings of love for Our Father in Heaven, and call upon the name of Jesus Christ.

2. Pray to Jesus Christ and ask that your sins be forgiven. Put the palms of your hands together in front of you at your heart level and say a prayer like this:

   Jesus Christ, of my own free will, I do renounce Satan, lucifer, the devil, all demons & hell. I am very grateful for all you have given my loved ones and me. Thank you for the many blessings you have given us. Thank you for your grace. You are the one true source of all creation and I only worship you. Please send the Holy Spirit to protect my loved ones and me from evil. I ask that my sins be forgiven. I am open to the guidance of the Holy Spirit. Truly.

3. Close your eyes. Visualize the Holy Spirit as if it were clear glowing water coming down from above. Imagine it entering into the top of your head. Imagine that you are filled and then surrounded by an aura of glowing light. Imagine that this aura expands into a sphere of light which surrounds you. You may direct this visualization with subvocalization. You might subvocalize something like this:

   I see the Holy Spirit flow into my crown as clear flowing water. I am filled with the Holy Spirit. I am surrounded with the Holy Spirit. Thank you Jesus Christ.

4. Write down a list of your sins. I'm not talking about a traditional religious view of sin. I'm not talking about rules or commandments that you've broken. But every person in the world has done things, or failed to do things, for which they regret. Perhaps you've done something that hurt somebody you loved. Perhaps you've hurt yourself. Perhaps there has been a situation where you've failed to be loving enough, or where you acted with insensitivity. This isn't something anyone else can decide for you. These are simply things that you know you've done wrong. Or things that you should have done but failed to do. Everyone makes mistakes. That's the human condition. This is not an intellectual exercise. Write this list from a heart level or a gut level.

5. Read the list out loud to Jesus and ask for your sins to be forgiven, knowing with faith that He will do so. Jesus Christ loves you as a parent loves his child, and He will always forgive you if you ask. You can do this in the presence of your study partner or some other trusted persons, but you don't need a human witness. You can do this alone in the presence of the Holy Spirit.

6. Burn the list in some safe way. Do this knowing that your sins have been forgiven. They have been washed away by the blood of Christ's sacrifice. So now you are free.

. Lesson Seventeen .

Some of the psychic Christians who developed this book were inspired by the life of Edgar Cayce, so it would be good to say a little about him. He lived from 1877 to 1945. He was a devoted Christian who taught Sunday school at one time. He read and reread the Bible throughout his life. He considered that the best way to become psychic was to become more spiritual. He was called the "sleeping prophet" because he apparently received psychic information while in a trance state. Much of the materials he produced were concerned with holistic health. Many people claim to have been helped by him. But many of the writings he produced were also considered to be controversial; there have been Christians who have criticized what they see as false doctrine contained in his writings.

There can be no doubt that many people were helped by the works of Edgar Cayce, and in a sense he is a role model for psychic Christians. But the psychic Christians who developed the system described in this book have a somewhat different intention for their work. They don't necessarily agree with all of the teachings of Edgar Cayce and they aren't interested in his trance-state technique for accessing psychic powers. What does interest them is to help ordinary people develop their own psychic powers. They want to teach people to use their psychic powers consciously when awake. The goal of this book isn't to create sleeping prophets but to awaken people to the power of their enhanced intuitive abilities.

lower vibrational psychic energy: *noun*, in this handbook this refers to psychic energies, arising from the Gaian life force, which are fear-based. These would be subjectively experienced as fear, anger, hate, greed and unhealthy sexual obsession.

higher vibrational psychic energy: *noun*, in this handbook this refers to love-based psychic energies, which may arise both from the Divine Energy Source as well as the Gaian life force. These would be subjectively experienced as love, joy, health, prosperity consciousness and healthy sexual attraction.

The Ethical Universe

Empathy is the essential principle of ethics. Empathy is a natural human instinct which is inborn. But this natural empathy can be lost through birth trauma, painful childhood experiences, a lack of bonding with parents or social training to eliminate empathy. Empathy may be limited in scope through social training so that a person may only extend empathy to other persons of a similar social background. In extreme cases, empathy may be completely trained out of a person's consciousness.

A Christian Biblical guideline says, "Do unto others as you would have them do unto you."

This is an encouragement for you to regain your natural

empathetic state of being. And the highest expression of empathy is love.

Love of self, love of romantic partner, love of family, love of tribe, love of humanity, love of life, love of God, these seven expressions of love all represent natural instincts. No matter how well life has allowed you to fulfill these instincts, by nature, all of these instincts are there. God has intelligently-designed us to feel and express love.

Intelligent Design is the theory that life didn't arise by random processes but was designed by an intelligent entity of some kind. Really this is the valid theory for the biological creation of life.

Darwinism is a flawed theory of biological evolution because it claims that one species can adapt itself into becoming an entirely new species. For example, according to Darwinism, primates of some kind, similar to monkeys, eventually became human beings evolving through chance processes a little bit at a time over very long periods of time. There is no actual evidence to support this, it is all conjecture and has no basis in empirical science.

The Book of Genesis is a beautiful poem, but it isn't a scientific description of creation; yet it is a very accurate metaphorical description of the creation process. *Creationism* is the theory that the *Book of Genesis* is literally true. Ironically, this comes closer to being in agreement with science than does Darwinism.

Intelligent Design isn't the same as Creationism, which demands a literal interpretation of the Bible. But Intelligent

Design does acknowledge that the cosmos, on an intrinsic level, is intelligent and conscious. In this sense, it acknowledges an aesthetic truth which is contained metaphorically in the *Book of Genesis*.

Think of the educational process of debate that has taken place in various forums over the years between the Darwinists and the Creationists. Yet debate of any kind creates a structured way of thinking; this is defined as the process which expresses *thesis, antithesis* and *synthesis*. This debating method has been used to teach students since the days of ancient Greece. The *Book of Genesis* is the basis for *Creationism* which demands a literal interpretation of the Bible; this was the original *thesis*. Darwinism came along with the *antithesis* to Creationism. The debates between the Creationists and the Darwinists has resulted in a *synthesis* of thought. Intelligent Design is the result of that synthesis.

Some proponents of Intelligent Design recognize that on subatomic levels of the cosmos there is the expression of intelligence and consciousness. So although Natural Selection may be one valid mechanism in the process of biological evolution, it's not the entire story. But actually, the theory of Natural Selection isn't the only possible explanation for the phenomenon of a species adaptation to environmental changes. Yet one must admit that Natural Selection might explain how a species can change forms to adapt itself to the environment. But the idea that one species can evolve through Natural Selection to eventually turn into an entirely different species has never been proven by any actual empirical evidence; it's all unproven conjecture.

Actually Darwin almost certainly conceived of this bizarre

idea through his study of esoteric and ancient religious texts. So this philosophy of Darwinism was always actually mysticism and never truly scientifically derived.

Quantum physics, which recognizes the significance of consciousness and interconnection, opens the door to understanding why life was intelligently designed. You need these advanced theories of Intelligent Design to explain the origins of DNA and the structure of complex cellular mechanisms.

I am not denying the possibility that Creationism, which interprets the *Book of Genesis* in a literal way, may be valid in some way. The problem is that some Creationists have turned the *Book of Genesis* into a false god claiming that you must accept a literal belief in it or be damned. But the Genesis story has never been completely validated by scientific data.

In actuality, true Christianity doesn't require that you believe in a literal interpretation of the *Book of Genesis* or the Old Testament. As a Christian, you are only required to believe in Jesus Christ.

Jesus the Nazarene was a man of history. He did exist. Personally I believe that the miracles written of in the Gospels literally took place as described. Some Christians consider, however, that the New Testament is a combination of both historical fact and mythological stories. I personally have no quarrel with such Christians. What you need to realize to be a follower of Jesus Christ is that he literally did die on the cross. He made this sacrifice out of love. And God has spoken to humanity through Christ's teachings.

Christ's teachings eliminate all of the rules and dogma of the Old Testament as well as the dogma of other religions and non-religious philosophies. The law of God is *love*. With this one word, Jesus has taught us the law.

But although I have a literal belief in the miracles performed by Jesus, I do recognize that most of His teachings were parables and poetic metaphors, not to be taken literally. Those Christian ministers who demand that you must interpret the Bible in a literal way are trying to create a new dogma to imprison their followers. But you don't have to follow their dogma to be a Christian, you only have to follow Jesus Christ and believe in His law of love.

As a Christian, you don't have to deny the validity of scientific fact. Many scientists and scholars who have studied the death and resurrection of Jesus Christ have concluded that it is a factual historical event. But this is not the case for all of the stories in the Old Testament, many of which may be legitimately viewed as a combination of metaphorical teachings set on a backdrop of historical events. Personally I believe that many of the stories in the Old Testament were inspired by historical events, as remarkable as that may seem. But the important aspect of the Old Testament is the story it tells of humanity's fall from God's grace and how a people struggled to return to that grace. This is the story of the human condition told through the stories of a specific group of people. It doesn't matter if their stories were literally true. It's our identification with their spiritual struggles that matter. So to demand a literal interpretation of the Old Testament stories only creates a distracting argument.

So you don't have to accept Creationism in order to be a

Christian; you can accept it or reject it; but if you care about scientific factuality, you do need to reject the scientism of Darwinism.

Your recognition that there is an intelligent designer of life does not require that you accept a literal interpretation of the Bible. Some people believe that on a subatomic foundational level of the cosmos, the cosmos itself manifests the qualities of intelligence and consciousness. So it could be that it is an *intelligent and conscious cosmos* that is designing life through subatomic processes which scientists will never directly observe.

What this has to do with ethics is this: Darwinism describes a process for Creation without intention and without moral judgement; Intelligent Design puts morality and intention back into the equation. Human beings were not the creation of some amoral and unintentional process. Social Darwinism with its rejection of morality is insane and destructive to civilization. There is a Creator of humanity. This Creator intends that we be moral. We live in an ethical universe. This is why ethics actually matter.

The Ethics of a Psychic Christian

Feeling empathy and seeking an understanding for the viewpoint of others is the basis of all ethics, however the specific ethics of being a psychic Christian is five-fold:

1. Reject the deceptive techniques of the psychic frauds.
2. Make spiritual love the basis of all your psychic practices.

3. Reject psychic practices based on materialistic attitudes or lower vibrational energies.
4. Teach what you know openly to those who are receptive.
5. Never worship false gods or invoke demons; only worship Our Father in Heaven in spirit.

Contemporary skeptics deny the validity of psychic abilities and in doing so demonstrate a lack of insight; however, even the mundane skeptics aren't wrong about everything. Some people claiming to be psychics are fraudulent. There are many different techniques that frauds may use to fake psychic abilities. But these break down into three categories:

1. Cold reading
2. Telling people what they want to hear
3. Trickery

Cold reading consists of getting people to give information about themselves so that the faker can pretend to have gotten that information through psychic methods. A faker might say something vague like, "I'm picking up that someone connected to you gave somebody a calendar as a gift." Of course, calendars are very popular gifts, and it's a safe bet that the victim of psychic fraud will respond in some way. So, for example, when the victim replies that his late uncle once gave a calendar to his elderly mother, the faker has his hooks into the victim. The faker may then say something like, "I'm sensing that your uncle, on the other side, is trying to reach us. He's saying that he wants you to pray for your mother's health." This is what the cold readers do, they tease information out of people through covert methods. When people play along with this game, the illusion of psychic ability may be created.

Many people who contact psychic frauds want answers to certain typical questions. They want to know that their loved-ones who have passed on are in Heaven. They are looking for romance. They have concerns about money. Those fakers who can only pretend to have psychic abilities have no real answers, but they know what people want to hear. So if you're calling somebody on a hotline who is faking psychic abilities, you're going to get their standard answers no matter what questions you ask.

There are all types of tricks and illusions by which psychic ability may be faked. For example, a faker might see what you've written on a piece of paper by looking at the reflection in a window behind you. Then there's spoon bending. If you take a silver spoon and weaken it by bending it back and forth, as you then hold it in your hand, the body heat from your hand will soften the metal to the point where it will seem to bend on its own. There are hundreds of tricks of this sort. When examining claims of psychic abilities, it's good to have a healthy regard for critical thinking. However, more than that, once you've developed your own psychic ability, you'll be able to intuitively sense when other people are either being real or faking it. As a psychic, you can feel when others are using their powers.

Furthermore, psychic powers are subtle and yet real. Telekinesis can be used to promote healing in another person on the other side of the world, but you can't use it to pull a rabbit out of hat. Once you've developed psychic powers you'll know what's possible and what isn't. But ethics demands that you be honest with yourself and others about your abilities.

There are some persons, trying to make money as professional psychics, who have learned to develop a limited level of psychic ability, and thus they try to combine fraudulent techniques with authentic ones. This is where ethics come in. Whenever people fake psychic abilities, they encourage the mundane skeptics to deny their own potential for authentic psychic abilities. So it's best to be honest with people and not pretend a level of psychic power you don't actually possess.

You must found your psychic practices on feelings of love, not fear. Through spirituality, you are connected to other people. If you direct negative thoughts toward people you can only create bad experiences for yourself. It's best to start off feeling empathy for people and direct love-based, positive thoughts towards people. That way you'll create good experiences for yourself. You need to realize that your thoughts aren't just abstract ideas. Your thoughts are energetic. Your thoughts direct your psychic energy.

However, this is a subtle force. Suppose you get angry with a friend and think, "I wish you were dead." That thought won't kill him, and if he dies soon after it won't be because of your fleeting, unkind thought. But if you direct focused and repeated negative thoughts toward a person over a period of time, it could cause actual harm to him and you. This isn't a superstitious belief, it's quantum physics applied to psychology. With psychic training your thoughts become more intensified and focused. The thought-energy put out by a psychic is greater than the thought-energy put out by a mundane-thinking person. This is why it's an ethical responsibility of a psychic Christian to have a persistent attitude of good will for all people.

This is the problem with the occult dabblers, they have enough knowledge of psychic power to do some harm, but not enough knowledge to do good. I feel sad when I think about how misguided medieval Christians would burn witches at the stake. And I feel no ill-will toward modern Wiccan members. But I recognize that it can be dangerous to dabble with forces that one does not truly understand. Satanic occultists who have read some books on witchcraft may try to use them to experiment with psychic powers with the intention of achieving unethical goals, and this can cause problems.

Typically occultists cast spells to fulfill their greed, lust or desire for revenge. You have to be very careful about your intentions. It's perfectly ethical to have the intention to achieve prosperity; but you must include in that intention the desire to achieve prosperity in ethical ways. Greed is driven by a fear of lack. Prosperity consciousness is driven by a love of self and others as well as a sense of gratitude for all that God has given you. It's perfectly ethical to use your psychic abilities to attract the type of relationship that your good heart desires; but this is never about manipulation. You should never use psychic abilities with the intention of harming another person. Emotions such as fear, anger or hatred are a part of the human condition and everyone feels them at one time or another. But you must never ritualistically direct your psychic projections based on such negative feelings. When you ritualistically evoke your psychic powers you must always be centered in feelings of love, serenity and gratitude to God.

When occult dabblers use their psychic practices while

experiencing negative emotions they harm themselves and others with their projections of lower vibrational psychic energy. Psychic Christians reject this type of unethical use of psychic power. Creating a psychic shield doesn't harm those persons who are attacking you, a psychic shield only defends yourself and others. A strong psychic shield will automatically dispel the lower vibrational energies projected toward you or those you intend to protect; in this way you can defeat any troublesome occult dabblers. Later lessons teach more techniques for strengthening your psychic shield.

Psychic Christians can afford to be honest about their practices when speaking with open-minded persons, but occult practitioners tend to be secretive when they have unethical intentions. One reason that this handbook was released was to openly present knowledge on ethical psychic practices so that interested persons wouldn't be tempted to go down the path of occultism. If you really understand psychic power then you won't use it for greed, or lust, or any shameful purpose; psychic ability is only empowering if it's used with ethical good will for all.

Training Practice

Ethical behavior is not about memorizing rules to be obeyed; to be fully ethical is to be fully loving. The learning drill for this section is to contemplate the nature of love. Take a big sheet of paper and draw a small seven pointed star at the center. This will represent the seven natural expressions of love. At the seven points write these words: *self, romance, family, fellowship, humanity, life* and *God*. Then around the page, in no particular order, depict the expressions of love which are most relevant to you. You can use words, quotes, symbols, and drawings. It's your contemplation of the nature of love, not the piece of paper, that matters. This is a meditation on the subject of love which you will write and draw onto paper. You may wish to keep this piece of paper so that you can meditate upon it in the future. The more you are able to focus your thoughts on love, the more harmonic you become with God. When you are centered in love, you are naturally ethical. As a psychic Christian, it's vital that you base your practices on feelings of love. So as you develop your psychic abilities, be sure to do this type of contemplation of love on a regular basis.

. Lesson Eighteen .

The intuitive mind is a sacred gift and the rational mind is a faithful servant. We have created a society that honors the servant and has forgotten the gift. We will not solve the problems of the world from the same level of thinking we were in when we created them. More than anything else, this new century demands new thinking; we must change our materially based analyses of the world around us to include broader, more multidimensional perspectives.
Albert Einstein

Self Esteem and Media Mind Control

self: the unified soul, mind, and body.

personality: For the purposes of this handbook, the personality is defined as the persona, the core personality, and the shadow personality.

The *persona* is the social role that you wear like a mask in dealing with people in society. In dealing with society, everyone is like an actor, playing a certain social role. There is the persona of your job, the persona of your day-to-day dealings with people, and the persona that you wear when you're having fun. Having a persona allows you to better interact with people and it protects you emotionally. To some extent, your persona is disconnected from your core emotions and thus it protects your emotional self.

However, you have to share your real emotions with the people you care about. Sometimes you have to take off the social mask of the persona and allow yourself to be emotionally vulnerable. This is your *core personality*.

Nevertheless, there are some emotions and thoughts that you don't share with anyone. Of course Jesus Christ knows everything you think and feel, so you're never really alone. But in living your life, you've probably learned that some emotions and thoughts are better kept to yourself. If you suppress your thoughts and feelings too much this could drive you insane. But nobody is so open that they share everything. Any aspect of your personality that you hide is your *shadow personality*.

Your persona is known to everyone. Your core personality is known to your closest friends and family. Your shadow personality is known only to yourself and Jesus. And it could be said that Jesus Christ knows you better than you know yourself.

Personality is the means through which you interact with the world. Your persona is a model of your inner self which you present to the world. Your core personality is a model of your inner self which you present to your loved ones. Your shadow personality is a model of your inner self which you withhold from the world.

Sometimes there are good reasons for withholding certain

things you feel or think. For example, persons who continually obsess on their anger aren't really being honest, they're being self-indulgent. Sometimes part of being an adult is knowing what you need to withhold. Even when you feel angry, sometimes it's best to keep it inside until you can find a way to process it or let it go. Your shadow self isn't evil, it's just that which must be withheld.

However, as you develop psychic powers, you may sometimes come to realize that you can safely let out aspects of your shadow self which you have been withholding. As you achieve a greater psychic connection with other people, you may come to realize that some of the things which you have kept secret may be safely shared with others. In this way you can let some of your shadow personality out into the light.

Sometimes negative emotions which you've withheld to protect others may make you sick if you don't find a way to process them. If you feel a great deal of unexpressed anger, you may be able to learn to find healthy ways to express it. Emotions are energy, and energy can be given new forms. Negative emotions aren't evil, they're just energies which haven't yet found an appropriate outlet. Some activities sublimate emotional energies, such as sports. As you come to realize fully who you are as a personality, you come to realize better ways interact with the world. You do this by figuring out how you can best express your many energies.

If you withhold that which is within you, it might destroy you. But if you find a way to express that which is within you, it may save you. Within you is an entire world of your own creation. Understanding this truth is essential to psychic ability.

One of the great secrets revealed by neurology is that the individual isn't directly perceiving reality with his or her senses. The brain takes in sensory perception as raw data, it constructs a model of reality based on that raw data, and then the consciousness of the individual views this model of reality. What you are looking at when you look at a rose isn't your visual perception of a rose, it's your brain's construct of a rose. Of course the brain is constantly receiving raw data from the senses, so it's a construct of reality that is constantly updated.

This is why you can see optical illusions. This is why you can see hallucinations. Some of the great intellectuals of the 1950s experimented with LSD, and some saw it as a path to enlightenment. Long before that, shaman used natural hallucinogenic drugs for mind-expanding purposes. This handbook doesn't recommended this as a part of your psychic training, but if you've ever seen a hallucination, you have learned something important, whether you've realized its significance or not. What a hallucination proves is that this model of reality given to you by the brain can contain lies. When the brain's construction of reality is altered in some significant way by hallucination, it reveals this truth. There's actually a bigger reality out there than the one that's presented to you by the constructed model of reality created by the brain. But you don't need to take drugs to know this truth.

The whole purpose of propaganda and brainwashing is to alter the individual's model of reality. By redefining the individual's model of reality, manipulative persons can redefine the individual's self-image. And we live in a time when propaganda and mind control are rampant. This is one of the biggest barriers you face in developing your psychic ability. The entire contemporary culture works to condition people to believe that there's no such thing as psychic ability. People are born with natural psychic abilities, but the average person has been brainwashed or socialized to suppress them. Fictional movies and sci-fi stories present psychic power in unrealistic ways, and often it's presented as a curse in which the fictional psychic can't control or even understand his powers. Yet psychic powers are real and they're not evil. The truth is, you don't know who you really are until you develop your psychic powers. Until then, you are living inside a false model of reality.

Attack on the self-esteem of the individual in this contemporary culture is never-ending. You can never be thin enough, strong enough, handsome enough, sexy enough or rich enough. The images presented to you on television are always unattainable. Men are made to feel that they should be super-heroes with unattainable superhuman abilities. Women are made to feel that they should be supermodels with unattainable glamor. No matter what you achieve at work, it isn't enough. You can't be productive enough. Dogmatic church leaders tell you that you were born in sin instead of telling you that you're a child of God. No matter what you accomplish, you'll never be good enough. Your salary will never be enough to pay your bills or to make sure that you have all the expensive toys advertised on television. You're in a rat race. You are being manipulated like a lab rat in a maze. And the mechanism for manipulating you is an image of yourself which can never be achieved. Until you escape the false model of reality that this materialistic culture is projecting upon your consciousness, you will never escape the trap of being mundane.

This is a story that mundane society has told you about psychic ability; they've told you that it's all a fraud. The contemporary king-Skeptic who is quoted time and time again as the man who has disproved all psychics is the so-called Amazing Randy, who is not an actual scientist but merely a Las Vegas stage entertainer.

If you go into enough research you'll find that time and time again scientists have shown that psychic abilities do exist. The US Defense Department spent more than twenty million dollars over more than twenty-five years doing psychic research and running a functioning psychic warfare unit. They did this because they knew that psychic abilities do in fact exist. The Stanford Research Institute, SRI, devoted considerable resources to such research, and congressional hearings proved that there were examples of their successes.

However, real-world psychic abilities don't express themselves in dramatic ways such as you might see on some silly TV movie. Real psychic abilities are subtle. Things like spoon bending and levitation are obviously not real. But remote healing and remote viewing can take place, and science has proven this. So you have a choice, you can believe the hard science or you can believe in a Las Vegas stage entertainer.

If you have realistic expectations for your psychic powers, you can develop them so that they serve you. Once you have developed them, you won't need faith because you'll have experience. But there's a great deal of effort that's been put out through the educational system and the mass media which encourages you to have low self esteem as well as a limited awareness of your own powers. So you should know that the realistic development of your psychic power is an authentic expression of your self esteem. You have a right to these powers as well as your self esteem.

Psychic powers don't have to be expressed consciously for them to work to your advantage. This is a very important point. When psychic abilities are directed by your superconscious levels of mind, they may serve your life in extraordinary ways. You do this by developing your spirituality.

Spiritual development isn't always just about worship, prayer and meditation. To spend time out in the natural world is a spiritual experience. Creating joyful experiences with pets, friends and family can enhance your natural spirituality. To be spiritual is to appreciate the beauty of the world and to walk within that beauty.

You can attune your conscious mind to your subconscious mind with certain practices. When you do this you will find that your conscious mind can indirectly guide your psychic powers. Your subconscious mind interacts with your superconscious mind to evoke your psychic powers. In this way they will automatically serve you to create a better life.

What I mean by this is that you can develop a useful interaction between your conscious mind and your subconscious mind. You can make conscious choices which protect your subconscious mind from negative influences.

The key to doing this is to take back control of your

imagination from the television set and the media propaganda. You need to take back your natural power of visualization. *Mechanical visualization projectors*, such as TV and videos, hijack this power. If you watch a lot of television or play video games a great deal, you should consider cutting back. Most contemporary news programs on TV are little more than propaganda. It's better to study current events through reading. If you do watch videos, think carefully about what you watch.

Everything you look at influences your subconscious mind. This handbook suggests that you avoid looking at videos depicting graphic violence or sexual perversion.

I know that for many people looking at videos is a social activity, so it might be unreasonable to demand that you stop completely. But you can cut back some during your basic psychic training. And you can choose to look at positive, life-affirming videos instead of trash. Comedies are better than horror. Family-oriented movies are better than porn. When you look at garbage on the screen, you are pouring garbage into your subconscious mind.

Also the lyrics of popular music tend to act like hypnotic suggestions, but because such lyrics tend to be nonsensical, listening to pop music tends to create confusion on a subconscious level of mind. So while you're training yourself to develop psychic abilities you might consider avoiding music that has lyrics to it and to instead listen only to instrumental music.

gray screen: This is a neutrally colored blank space that you can stare at. You can use a middle gray poster board with no designs or patterns on it. You can use an ordinary blank wall space that has been painted in a neutral color such as white, gray or brown. You can hang a ordinary piece of gray cloth about the size of a TV screen on the wall. A gray towel will do. Basically this is just a blank space that you can gaze at while do certain types of opened-eyed meditations.

Training Practice

Gray screen gazing is used for the purposes of psychic stimulation. By keeping your eyes open, you avoid inviting imagination into your mind. By staring at a neutrally colored blank space, you keep your mind blank, that is, open and receptive. *Gray screen gazing* is a psychic practice that can be used in a number of ways. It's a basic technique for making yourself psychically receptive. Your visual cortex connects left and right hemispheres. By keeping your eyes open, and looking at a blank, neutrally colored space, you invite psychic information to go from your subconscious into your conscious mind.

If you sit in a comfortable chair with ear plugs in yours ears and gaze at a gray screen it can be a mild form of sensory deprivation. Under such conditions, some psychics see faint visualize impressions on the gray screen, or even hear words, but that's not really the point of this practice.

The use of gray screen gazing is to create mental openness. If you pray to Jesus Christ and then gaze at a gray screen, you can pay attention to your thoughts and intuitively sense which thoughts are being guided by the Holy Spirit. Some Christians pray to Jesus Christ for guidance, but then don't leave any room in their thoughts for Him to respond. In effect, by gazing at a gray screen you are making your mind open to Christ's guidance through the Holy Spirit.

While doing this particular training practice, you may wish to play relaxing instrumental music in the background. Before practicing this, center yourself in your love for God with prayer.

This is the practice combining praising affirmation with open-eyes mediation that follows closed-eyes visualization. It will follow a cycle of *praise, visualization* and *gray screen gazing*.

First sit in a comfortable position in front of a gray screen. Gently look at it in an unfocused way, scan over this blank space briefly, looking up and down at it.

Then subvocalize saying, "Praise Lord Jesus Christ. I am open to the Holy Spirit."

Next close your eyes and create with your imagination a brief daydream. Visualize something that you desire to achieve in your life. Imagine something in your life and the lives of your loved ones as you would wish it to be. Or you can visualize something that concerns you.

You can support your visualization with subvocalization.

For example if you want greater wealth, while visualizing you might subvocalize by saying things like, "I see myself with greater wealth. I see my bank account statement with large amounts of money in it."

Your visualized wishes don't have to be realistic. Furthermore, in making a visualization you should know that the thing you wish for won't necessarily magically come about. But don't worry about being realistic. Don't censor your desires.

If you want wealth, visualize that. If you want to a loving relationship, visualize that. Visualize the changes you want to see in the political system. Or visualize concerns that you have in your life.

Your subconscious mind will respond in some positive way to any visualization. Your subconscious mind is strongly linked to your superconscious mind, and your superconscious mind is the source of your psychic power. So trust the superconscious mind to respond in some positive way to your visualization.

However, I'm not saying that by visualizing the things you desire they will come about. In fact you shouldn't demand that your visualizations become realized in the world. Each visualization is a communication, a statement made to your superconscious mind. Instead of fulfilling your desires, your superconscious mind might respond to the visualization by encouraging you to modify your desires. So after you close your eyes and visualize, you need to open your eyes and become receptive to a response from your superconscious mind.

After you briefly visualize this wish, open your eyes and look at the gray screen again. You may or may not sense images or forms in the blank space that you are looking at. But just gaze at the blank space for a brief period of time. In gazing at the gray screen you are making your mind open to the Holy Spirit. Pay attention to any thoughts that occur to you. Gaze at the gray screen for perhaps as long as half a minute. Don't worry if nothing significant occurs to you. What's important here is your willingness to be open to the Holy Spirit.

Then close your eyes gain and subvocalize, "Praise Lord Jesus Christ. I am open to the Holy Spirit."

While your eyes are still closed, again visualize something that you'd like to achieve or some concern. It can be the same thing or something else.

Continue with this cycle of praise, visualization and gray screen gazing for as long as you feel comfortable.

You may find that you experience insights as you go through this process. You may feel a sensation of love in your heart center.

Do this practice whenever you feel in the mood to do so. It will consecrate your subconscious and superconscious psychic powers to the service of your life.

But never use hateful visualizations. Don't base any visualization on anger. Don't allow any negativity into any of these visualizations. All visualization must be based on higher vibrational energies. If you find yourself dwelling on lower vibrational energies as you attempt this practice, stop doing this practice and do something else. Only use this practice when you feel naturally centered on feelings of serenity and spiritual love.

But there is a point about this drill that should be made. It may seem unrealistic to think that you can change the minds of political leaders. But if enough people visualize such changes, it will begin to change the thinking of those in power. In fact, in the future of this world, this will be how politics works. The people will awaken to their ability to psychically influence their leaders, and they will use this power to direct the political leaders to serve the will of the people. I point this out because I know of some Christian psychics who use this visualization technique above to psychically influence political leaders to do the right thing. And they also receive political insights while doing this.

. Lesson Nineteen .

Peace I leave with you, my peace I give unto you: not as the world giveth, give I unto you. Let not your heart be troubled, neither let it be afraid.

John 14:27

Prayer and Meditation

You should have realistic expectations for your psychic abilities. In fantastical sci-fi movies, people with psychic abilities are depicted as having supernatural powers. They can kill people with their telekinesis and fly through the air, things of that sort. Real-world psychic training focuses on abilities such as the development of clairvoyant insight and remote healing through prayer. Clairvoyance is the ability to use subtle psychic insights to enhance the powers of reason. This gives the clairvoyant individual tremendous advantages over those who have not developed their power of intuition. As you learn to use prayer to heal yourself and others you will see and experience the results. You should expect that if you develop your psychic abilities you will be able to live a better life. This is because you will have greater self determination and certainty in your decision making. It's this self determinism and certainty which defines the lifestyle of the psychic Christian.

But this clairvoyant lifestyle should not be underestimated. Many people live their lives in a fog of uncertainty; they feel that they are pulled back and forth by external forces which they don't control. The clairvoyant lifestyle of the psychic Christian leads the individual to feel that he or she is back in control of his life, and it creates a clear sense of purpose.

When and how often you pray and meditate may also be determined by both personal desire and practical considerations. However, during the time when you are developing your psychic ability, it is recommended that you practice prayer and meditation (of some kind) at least twice a day, everyday. After you have completed this course, you can reevaluate how often you need to do this.

Although a specific prayer and mantra will be suggested below, what prayer and mantra you use should be a personal choice. What is most important is that any prayer or mantra you use be representative of your spiritual love for God. Prayer and meditation is a way to center your life in an awareness of yourself as a child of God.

The most important aspect of prayer is that you are centered in a feeling of gratitude for God's many blessings; your feelings of gratitude matter more than any ritualistic aspect of prayer. However, there is something to be said for the ritualistic use of a traditional prayer position. The traditional prayer position is to kneel or sit and to bring the palms of the hands together at the heart level with the head tilted slightly forward and eyes closed. Knee problems, or other practical reasons, might make the act of kneeling unreasonable. Yet if the prayer can be said while in the traditional prayer position, it may be more effective. This traditional prayer position mimics the position of the embryo in the womb. To assume that position while saying the prayer brings forth positive feelings associated with prenatal memory.

Follow prayer with the practice of mantra meditation. It is suggested that you use this technique:

While sitting in a comfortable position with eyes opened, you concentrate upon subvocalizing a spiritual mantra. While physically still, gaze in a comfortable way at a blank space. Ideally this blank space would be a gray area such as a gray wall or a middle gray cloth hung on a wall. Blink as necessary. Don't concern yourself if your mind's eye creates images in the blank space, just let them go. Blink your eyes as needed. Make your gaze a soft one. Repeatedly subvocalize the mantra while in a state of calmness. This will open your mind to the Holy Spirit. Insights into your relationship with Jesus Christ may fill your mind. Or you may simply feel the peace of God as you meditate in this way. When mundane thoughts enter into the mind which distract from the mantra or from your serenity, acknowledge such thoughts and then return to the repeating of the mantra. It's important to remain connected to your feelings of spiritual awareness while meditating.

You evoke your feeling of connection to God with the prayer and then you extend that feeling of connection with mantra meditation. Prayer and meditation is all about creating a spiritual awareness and then maintaining it for a time.

How long you meditate should be determined by practical considerations as well as emotional sensitivity. You should meditate for as long as it feels good to meditate.

Training Practice

Use the prayer and mantra below, or another prayer and mantra of your own choice, and actually practice prayer and meditation.

Prayer

Heavenly Parent,
Hallowed is your name.
Thy dominion come, Thy will be done,
on Earth as it is in Heaven.
Send to us the Spirit of Truth.
Bless us with the Holy Spirit.
Bestow to each a heart of courage,
That leads us our greatest good.
And may we be gracious with one another,
as Christ has been gracious with us.
For yours is the glory and power forever, Verily.

Mantra

God is Love.

. Lesson Twenty .

Several decades before writing this book, I developed some health issues. At that time in my life I was still naive in that I automatically trusted what I was told on news broadcasts; also I didn't question the advice given to me by medical doctors.

When GMO foods first came on the market, the news journalists commonly claimed that such foods were safe. Some GMO foods were more affordable, I had a limited food budget, thereby some GMO foods became a part of my diet.

After a while I began to develop a pain in my chest. I went to a doctor who misdiagnosed the problem and gave me a series of tests to see if I had a heart problem. These tests were very costly. One of the tests was dangerous and left me with permanent harm. Many thousands of dollars later, the doctors decided that the chest pains weren't being caused by a heart problem. The chest pains were caused by acid reflux. By then I had severe stomach problems and was violently throwing up my meals. So it was obvious that it had been a digestive problem all along. I lost weight rapidly and experienced severe stomach pains. The expensive doctors gave me various drugs which only made things worse.

They sent me to a specialist who did more expensive tests.

Thousands of dollars later, he was able to tell me that my symptoms weren't psychosomatic and that he had other patients who were experiencing the same problems. But he didn't know what was causing it, and he had no cures.

Through trial and error I figured out, on my own, what foods made me sick and which foods didn't. I had a small list of foods I could safely eat, so I stuck to them.

After more than a year of this, my health was diminishing because my diet was too restrictive. I wasn't getting all of the nutrients that I needed. I reached a crisis point where I knew that doctors couldn't help me.

When I had been younger, I had known some secretive persons who had demonstrated psychic abilities. But I hadn't seen any of them in years. Then when my health crisis reached this critical point, an old friend named James showed up.

He told me of this group he had heard of, who had been using psychic abilities to diagnose health problems. I had them do a reading for me. These psychics recommended that I avoid all GMO foods. They indicated that the GMO foods had caused the problem. They recommended that I drink Kombucha tea. I followed their advice and instantly experienced relief. Those health issues never came back. I became healthier directly as a result of that psychic health reading.

Growing up, I was told by my parents and my teachers at school that I should trust what doctors told me and that I should trust what I read in newspapers or see on the TV news. I was also told that I should distrust anyone who claimed to be a psychic because they were all fakers and frauds.

However, when I had my health crisis, my worldview was turned upside down. I realized that sometimes it's the doctors who are the fakers and frauds. I realized that sometimes the news media corporations give out false information. I also realized that sometimes the people who claim to use psychic powers are telling the truth.

Discernment

It's true that there are some psychic frauds. There are persons who claim to have psychic powers or healing powers but who are really fakers or con artists. But there are also some persons who have legitimate psychic abilities. There are legitimate spiritual healers. I would encourage you to develop the ability to discern between the fraudulent spiritual healers and the legitimate ones.

It's also true that you have the potential to be a spiritual healer because everyone is born with this power.

holistic health: This is the healing of the whole person: body, mind, emotions and spirit. Medical doctors often treat the injured body as if it were a broken machine to be fixed. Sometimes medical doctors do acknowledge psychology, but often they ignore the importance of spirituality. So spiritual healing is an important aspect of holistic health.

The first principle of spiritual healing is that you must decide to take responsibility for your health. This is not to say that it's your fault if you've gotten sick or been hurt in an accident. Taking responsibility isn't the same as blaming yourself. Taking responsibility means that you choose to do whatever is necessary to improve your health.

People often do things that make themselves ill, sometimes without realizing how. In this contemporary society, public information about medical issues and diet are often misleading. For example, many people don't realize that, rather than preventing illness, some vaccines are actually designed to make you sick.

If you wish to remain healthy in this unhealthy contemporary society, you must dedicate yourself to doing research. You have to do a great deal of research to know what foods are safe to eat and are good for you. Sometimes a simple change in diet can improve your health.

In recent years, there has been a consolidation of the corporations which control the news. At one time mainstream journalists had more integrity than they do right now. These days the decisions about what will be presented in the news are made by a relatively small group of people, none of whom care about anything other than corporate profits. Contemporary mass-media news sources are often deliberately inaccurate. Unfortunately, in this present time culture, you can't trust information from the government or the corporate-controlled news programs. You have to do your own research into issues.

Even information given to you by doctors may sometimes be inaccurate because they too are subjected to a corruptive corporate system.

We're not telling you these truths to make you paranoid, this is simply the way things are right now.

But even in the future, after society has been reformed, citizens will still be responsible to be educated in health issues. So it will always be true that you must take responsibility for your own health by doing your own research. Whether you are trying to maintain your health or to restore your health, you have to do a great deal of research. You have to research about healthy food and water. You have to educate yourself on basic health issues. You have to use your study skills as a first step in achieving or maintaining health.

Here are a few examples of how contemporary misinformation is making people ill. GMO foods are promoted as being safe when in fact they may cause illness. Psychiatric drugs are being widely promoted as a way of treating mental illness when in fact the over-prescribing of them has often harmed mental health. Circumcision is being promoted as being good for the health of male infants when in actuality it's a form of torture which causes severe health problems; furthermore, circumcision decreases sexual gratification when the victim grows to manhood.

Don't take my word for any of this, do your own in-depth research. But don't merely accept what you are told by authority figures. To be healthy, you need to rise above society's present status quo.

Another way to take responsibility for your health is to make the changes in your behavior which you know will improve your health. Certain things are obviously harmful like smoking cigarettes or failing to get appropriate exercise.

Until you choose to take responsibility, you will continue to be a victim of health problems, and your recovery simply will not take place.

There are many different systems of holistic health, and this handbook doesn't go into most of them. But there is one type of holistic health practice which does relate to psychic ability. This is the use of the Holy Spirit (Divine Source Energy) to heal oneself or others. You invoke this power when you pray for yourself or others.

Palm Healing

This is a type of spiritual healing where you project healing energy through the palms of your hands.

Through prayer you can evoke the Holy Spirit to send subtle healing energy to another person who is at a distance from you in space and/or time; however, Palm Healing, which can be done in person, can also be effective. Palm healing can be done in person by laying your hands on another person. Or it can be done at a distance by feeling the healing energy projected through your hands toward the person to be healed.

For example, you can write a person's name onto a piece of paper, and then place that piece of paper between your hands as you say a prayer for that person. And this will project the Divine Source Energy, through the palms of your hands, to the person being prayed for even if that person is miles away.

This would work like this, if you were praying for a friend named John Smith, you might say: *"Praise the Divine Source, all thanks to the Anointed Savior, we ask that Divine Source Energy be sent to my friend John Smith to miraculously heal him."*

Or you might say: *"Praise Our Father in Heaven, all thanks to Jesus Christ, we ask that the Holy Spirit be sent to my friend John Smith to miraculously heal him."*

Before saying such a prayer, if you were to write the name *"John Smith"* onto a piece of paper and hold it between the palms of your hands, this might increase the focus of your intention and make the prayer more powerful as a result. But you wouldn't even need to write his name onto the piece of paper, you could simply express the strong intention that he be healed. The name on a piece of paper would simply be an aid that helps you focus your mind.

Reiki practice is a version of Palm Healing, however, I'm not going to describe the Reiki method here in this lesson, if you want to learn more about Reiki you have to read about it on your own. I will tell you that some of the people who developed this system of psychic training were Christians who had studied Reiki healing. The Japanese system of Reiki healing really isn't a form of occultism. The founder of the Reiki healing movement in Japan was known to have studied Christianity. It's also true that two of the most important early organizers of the Reiki healing movement were openly Christian. Some Christians feel that Reiki practice is similar to the early Christian practice of laying hands on persons to heal them. However, you don't have to be a trained Reiki healer in order to do Palm Healing.

The bioenergy of your physical body is a part of the collective bioenergy of all of the lifeforms that make up the Earth's ecosystem. A scientist once named the collective activities of the ecosystem, calling it *Gaia* after an ancient Greek myth. This collective and energetic ecosystem contains its own intelligence and consciousness. A name for this phenomenon is the *Gaian life force*.

When Palm Healing is done in person, you're not just calling upon the Holy Spirit, you're also evoking the Gaian life force which is naturally projected by your own body. Furthermore there are psychological factors involved with Palm Healing which enhance its effectiveness when it's done in person rather than at a distance. When Palm Healing is done in person you place the palms of your hands onto another person to allow the natural Gaian life force to flow into that person's body.

Palm Healing is natural. Early Christians were known to perform healing through a "laying on of the hands." You find versions of this type of healing in cultures from all around the world. When a child is hurt, such as a skinned knee, the natural instinct of parents is to place their hands onto the hurt place. Your body naturally flows healing energy through the palms of your hands. If you take advantage of this fact, and you apply prayer and meditation to enhance the process, what you have is basic Palm Healing.

Gaian life force is continually being generated by your physical body. Gaian life force flows naturally out of the palms of your hands. Furthermore, the palms of your hands are sensitive in sensing the Gaian life force in others. The palms of your hands are almost like sensory organs; they receive information from the Gaian life force and they project the Gaian life force. If you were to place the palms of your hands onto the shoulders of another person, that person would naturally receive healing energy. Also, for emotional reasons, the friendly act of appropriately placing your hands on another person is psychologically beneficial. This is one reason why people shake hands and hug.

You can intensify the healing power of the natural Gaian life force with prayer by calling upon the Holy Spirit. Then the healing power of the Holy Spirit will complement and enhance the Gaian life force.

Think about where you can place the palms of your hands on another person's body so that it feels appropriate to that person as well as yourself.

Standing behind a person, who is sitting down, you may place the palms of your hands onto his or her shoulders.

Or you might place the palms of your hands onto the sides of his or her scalp.

If the person is lying down, you might place the palms of your hands onto that person's stomach, knees or ankles.

You would need to talk with the other person to determine that person's comfort zones as well as your own. In this type of simple Palm Healing, you would also use your intuition to determine where you place your hands and how long you keep them there.

Training Practice:
Palm Healing for Self Healing

Step 1. After washing your hands, sit in a comfortable chair, place the palms of your hands together at the heart level, close your eyes, and reverently call out to Jesus Christ for help.

Step 2. Say a prayer for healing. Word it anyway that seems appropriate to you, perhaps something like this.

> *Jesus Christ, Anointed Savior, thank you for all the blessings you have given me and my loved ones. I am grateful for my health. I am thankful for your unconditional love. Our Father in Heaven, Divine Source, you are the one true source of all creation and I worship you and you alone. I now open myself to your unconditional grace. Please send the Holy Spirit to me now. May Divine Source Energy flow forth from the palms of my hands.*

Step 3. Visualize the Holy Spirit entering into your body. With your eyes closed imagine that you see clear, glowing water, in the shape of a descending dove, flowing down from above entering into your body at the crown of your head. Imagine that this glowing force flows down into your heart level, then from there through your arms and out into the palms of your hands.

Subvocalization for visualization support:

> *The Holy Spirit, in the shape of a dove descends upon me from above. My mind and heart are open now. With my mind's eye, I see myself filled with glowing*

light. The Holy Spirit now flows from my hands like clear glowing water.

Step 4. It is preferable that you keep your eyes closed as you move your hands from place to place around your body.

However, you may need to open your eyes from time to time when you are learning the hand positions so that you can read this text. Once you memorize the hand positions you should be able to keep your eyes closed throughout this process.

Hand Positions: Take the palms of your hands and place them lightly on either side of your head so that your middle fingers touch at the crown of your head. Gently hold them there for a minute, remaining sensitive to your feelings. Next, move the palms of your hands around to your forehead with the fingers pointing upward, and hold them there in the same fashion for about a minute. Then, for about a minute place the palms of your hands gently on the sides of your neck. Don't apply pressure, just hold them there lightly. After that, lightly place your hands near your heart and hold them there gently for about a minute. Then do this with your stomach, holding your palms there for a minute or so. Next, place the palms of your hands on your hips for about a minute. Finally, place the palms of your hands on your knees for a minute or so.

Step 5. Open your eyes, and gently clap your hands about 7 times. (This will turn off the flow of Gaian life force and indicate the end of the healing session.) Finally, wash your hands again.

Note: Do this no more than twice a day, but repeat it as

often as you need to until you have memorized the process and can easily perform it. Do not move on to the next lesson until both you and your study partner can tangibly feel the Divine Source Energy flowing from the palms of your hands during self healing.

. LESSON TWENTY-ONE .

The Gospels tell the story of how Jesus Christ once healed the servant of an officer in the Roman army. This Roman Centurion came to Jesus asking him to heal his servant. Jesus agreed to do this and got up to go with the Centurion to his house. But the Roman soldier stopped him, indicating that he knew that Jesus could heal the man at a distance. Jesus marveled at the man's faith, and at that very instant the servant was miraculously healed.

Remote Healing

This phenomenon is also known as *healing at a distance*. There have been many controlled studies which show that ordinary prayer can be used to improve people's health conditions. The deeper the faith of the persons who pray, the more effective is the prayers. And the more people who pray the better. Prayer groups can significantly improve the health of their own members as well as others.

Training Drill: Send Healing Energy to your Study Partner

The *Sender* is the person who projects the healing energy

from the palms of his or her hands. The *Receiver* is the person who accepts the healing energy which is being projected by the Sender.

Healing energy can refer to the Gaian life force, Divine Source Energy or the combination of the two.

Divine Source Energy can be projected instantly to any location and to any time period. The distance involved (in space or time) does not influence the effectiveness of the healing power of the Divine Source Energy. Remarkably, Divine Source Energy is not limited by the dimension of time. You can send Divine Source Energy to comfort and heal a person in the past or in the future. For example, if you knew that a friend was going to undergo a surgical operation the next day, you could pray for your friend to receive healing energy during and after the operation, and the Divine Source Energy would heal him.

However, Gaian life force does involve bioenergy, and as such it has limits. Gaian life force can only be projected in the present time. And it can only be projected for short distances.

In this training practice, each of the two of you are to take turns sending and receiving healing energy. For the purposes of this training exercise, we're only interested in giving you a brief experience of sending the Gaian life force along with Divine Source Energy, to another person through palm healing. This experience will assist in a later training practice for telepathy.

The person receiving healing energy (the Receiver) sits in

a chair. The person sending healing energy (the Sender) starts off standing behind the Receiver's chair. Eventually the Sender will sit on a chair across from the Receiver, but in the first part of this practice the Sender stands behind the Receiver who is sitting down.

Always wash your hands before and after Palm Healing. This is common sense for sanitary reasons, but also this washing of the hands helps to ritualize the process, and that's always good in doing any type of psychic work. You want every process that you use for psychic ability to have the quality of ritual about it.

First, for this drill, evoke your awareness of God and say a prayer. Word this in whatever way feels appropriate to you.

Perhaps something like this:

> *Blessed is the Divine Source. In the name of the Anointed Savior may the Holy Spirit be called upon for the purpose of healing.*

After saying a prayer, place your hands gently on the shoulders of your study partner. After that, close your eyes.

Use use the psychic scanning method of scan/subvocalize/cognize in this way:

SCAN your study partner's body by imagining that you are beaming light into his or her body through the palms of your hands.

SUBVOCALIZE this affirmation: *I feel the flow of the Holy Spirit now.*

COGNIZE by paying attention to your feelings. Most people will feel a subtle flow of energy coming from their hands as they do this. That feeling is your cognition.

Repeat this pattern of scan/subvocalize/cognize a number of times, just to allow yourself to feel your connection to the Gaian life force and the Holy Spirit.

Then for the second part of this training practice, walk around so that you face the Receiver and sit in a chair a few feet away. Hold your hands up in front of you, face your palms forward and close your eyes. Imagine that beams of healing energy are projected from your palms to enter into your study partner's forehead. Try to see this with your mind's eye.

You will **SCAN** the Receiver by projecting healing energy. You won't be physically touching your study partner at this point. This will be remote Palm Healing.

Then **SUBVOCALIZE** the affirmation, *I feel the flow of healing energy now entering your forehead.*

COGNIZE: Then pay attention to the feelings in the palms of your hands for several seconds. That feeling in your palms will be your cognition.

Repeat this pattern of scan/subvocalize/cognize for a while. Use your intuition to determine how long you do this.

When you are done, gently clap your hands about 7 times. Then wash your hands.

After that you will switch roles with your study partner. The

Receiver becomes the Sender, and the Sender become the Receiver.

Do this training practice from this lesson no more than twice a day, and perform it with your study partner at least seven times before going on to the next lesson. So this will take at least a week, possibly longer, depending upon how often the two of you meet for practice.

. LESSON TWENTY-TWO .

It might be useful if you had some understanding of the history of the group of psychics who developed this system. Although I was responsible for wording their ideas and organizing the text, they were the ones who developed this system. Although I agree with their basic philosophy, these are their techniques and ideas, not mine. Resolute in their desire to remain anonymous, they have allowed this book be the only public expression of their basic psychic training course.

This is their story.

A friend of mine, who was known to me as James, was the last member of a secret society of heretical Christians. I have reason to believe that this group had been around since medieval times, but by the time of James it consisted of a handful of members all of whom were much older than him. They had a hidden library with old manuscripts which described esoteric techniques for psychic powers. They were very secretive, and many of their beliefs seemed odd.

James himself fell in love with a woman from outside of this group who believed in a more normal, traditional version of Christianity. So James lost interest in the more esoteric teachings of the secret society and became a more conventional Christian. But he retained his awareness that psychic powers were possible.

Eventually he met some other Christians who had been influenced by the works of Edgar Cayce as well as Reiki healing practice.

James and his Christian friends were aware of the existence of satanic occultists who cause great harm to this world. These Christians were interested in finding a way to combat the destructive psychic influence of satanic occultism.

Because their experiments with telepathy tended to be frowned down upon by many traditional Christians, the members of this group decided to maintain a state of secrecy, so as to avoid negative attention. James, who grew up in a secret society, knew how to structure a group for the purpose of maintaining secrecy. Because all of these Christians have social connections with one another, if even one member of the group were to become public, they would all be known, and this would create problems for many of them. So anyone joining their group had to promise to keep its existence a secret.

I am the only exception to that rule. Because nobody can connect me to James or the other group members, I was safe to use as their only public outlet for information. However, I'm not really a member of this group. In recent years I have met in private with James and dozens of other members. These meetings were conducted in such a way so that I could never learn the true identities of these people. So I do know that they are very careful about who they recruit into the group because of this need for secrecy.

Nevertheless, in spite of this limitation, they did expand their group's membership at one point in time. One day, a woman who was a member of this group happened to be reading a book by Edgar Cayce while sitting in a coffee shop. A man, who was ex-military, started up a conversation with her about psychic powers. It turned out that he had been a former member of the US Defense Department's psychic research program that had been conducted during the Cold War. Although she revealed nothing about her secret group, she saw a kindred spirit in the man. The two began dating. Eventually they fell in love and married. Because of this, he became a member of this secret Christian group, and he brought in other ex-military friends who had once been a part of the government's psychic research program.

This created a fusion of ideas and advancement of techniques. Because of this, many of the group's members came to develop significant levels of psychic ability. Some of the members used their psychic powers to attain wealth.

A "think-tank" is defined as a group of experts who gather to solve problems or develop new theories. This secretive group of Christians created a type of think-tank for psychic research. Over the years they have tried to improve upon their techniques for psychic development.

Although they wished to remain anonymous to the world, members of this group thought that some their ideas and methods should be made public. So they started to look for someone who could publish their ideas while respecting their desire to remain anonymous as individuals. That's where I came in. I was an old and trusted friend of James, and I had experience on the Radio as well as with publishing.

For reasons too complex to briefly explain, James and I had always kept our friendship secret, and James had always kept his identity a secret from me. I know that James was never his real name. I have never known where he lives or even what he does for a living. I talk about my friendship with James in other books, but I don't wish to go into all that now. I point this out only because it was my unique friendship with James that made me a the best candidate to be the public outlet for their system of psychic training.

I have published other versions of their basic psychic training course. This book is the most recent and final version. James died recently, and the group's new leader, Deborah, doesn't want to have any further contact with me after the publication of this revised version of the book. I understand her reasons for this, and I accept this group's need to remain anonymous.

Over the years, James and other members of this group trained me in my psychic development. My own psychic powers are rather limited. I'm not naturally talented when it comes to psychic powers. But the psychic powers that I have developed do serve me well. An empath can sense what other people are feeling even when they try to conceal it. I have become somewhat of an empath, which is strange because when I was younger I was devoid of empathy. Be warned that my psychic shielding techniques are as good as anyone's, and better than most. My intuitive insights have greatly improved my life. So I understand from personal experience how empowering it is to break through the psychic threshold.

You have reached a major Psychic Threshold

The purpose of this basic training course in psychic powers is to allow the individual to reach and transcend a *psychic threshold*. In a sense, mundane society has put you in a mental prison in which you are unaware of your psychic powers. The purpose of this course up until now has been to systematically weaken the walls of this prison. If you and your study partner can successfully complete the following lesson and training practice, you will break down the walls of that prison and be free to use your psychic abilities to empower your life.

Although the following training practice is highly formalized and structured, once you break through the psychic threshold, how you manifest your psychic abilities will not necessarily be structured in any particular way. Your latent psychic abilities are unique. So what they will be and how your will use them is something I can't predict for you.

Basic Telepathy and Divination Theory

The purpose of telepathy and divination isn't to do parlor tricks to amuse other people. This type of training has practical uses. Once you've had some experience with telepathic communication, even if it's a small experience, you'll find that your ordinary communication becomes more effective. In your conversations with people, you will be more empathetic. In your written communication you will be more insightful. As well as this, divination practice will make you better able to understand your purpose in life. You will become more intentional and effective in accomplishing your goals. Through divination practice, your relationship with the Holy Spirit will improve. This will cause you to be more confident in how you live your life.

In this system of psychic training, divination isn't an occult practice, it's a spiritual practice in which you are asking God to send you the Spirit of Truth. This is a different type of practice than the divination done by occult dabblers who open themselves to demonic influences. You must use divination with the attitude that you do so in service to Jesus Christ and humanity as well as your own enlightened self interests. For divination to work in this way, you must feel that you are in dynamic concordance with God.

Whatever tools you use for divination are not magical in and of themselves; a divination tool is any mechanism through which the subconscious mind, influenced by the superconscious mind, can express psychic insight. Divination is simply a way to receive guidance from the Spirit of Truth. Here, the Spirit of Truth is defined as the informational manifestation of the Holy Spirit. When such knowledge is revealed, you will apprehend it with a feeling of certainty. For some psychic Christians, divination tools aren't necessary because these psychics feel a strong connection to God. For them the Spirit of Truth is easily manifested into their awareness. Even if that turns out to be the case for you as well, some training that involves divination tools can be a useful way to condition your mind to be receptive to the Spirit of Truth.

A couple of examples of divination tools are playing cards or a forked stick for water dowsing.

Divination works by attuning your conscious mind to your subconscious mind so that the subtle movements of your physical hands are influenced directly by your superconscious mind. In this way the shuffling of cards or the bobbing of a stick becomes an expression of psychic ability.

Whatever divination tools you use should be consecrated to God before using them; in this way only the Spirit of Truth will speak through them. By spiritually consecrating your divination tools, you screen out negative psychic influences.

For example, if you're going to teach yourself dowsing, when you find or create an appropriate forked stick, say a prayer and ask God to bless the dowsing stick. Consecrate the dowsing stick to God by pledging to only use it for good purposes to help others.

In doing the training practices at the end of this lesson you'll need a standard playing card deck. Before you use this deck be sure to consecrate it with prayer. Strong intention determines your level of psychic power, so by consecrating your divination tools, you are expressing strong intention.

Astrology isn't evil, and it can be used for divination. The Old Testament verses that are used to condemn astrology are misunderstood because they are interpreted without an appropriate historical context. Bible verses taken out of context can be misleading. However, no form of divination should be used to impose limits upon persons or to compromise their power of free will. Good astrologers reveal options to their clients, they don't tell them their fate. With astrology you can come to understand the unseen influences in your life. Understanding such influences can help you to determine your own fate. Astrology is a complex discipline which is both a science and an art. It requires a great deal of study as well as a highly developed sense of intuition.

Contemporary astrologers vary greatly in terms of skill. If you consult an astrologer, you should locate a skillful one. And you shouldn't attempt to become a professional astrologer unless you are willing to do the study necessary.

What astrology describes is a psychological matrix that is being imposed upon you by the material universe. In reality, who you are as a person is determined by your spiritual relationship with God. For example, if you are under the sign of Leo, astrology may tell you that you desire to be the center of attention; but sometimes God might tell you that you need to be humble and let someone else be the center of attention. If you are aware of yourself as a child of God, then you are not a slave to your astrological chart. It may simply indicate worldly challenges that exist for you to overcome.

In Lesson 23, which comes after this lesson, you are going to deal with the simplest form of divination. This is where you mentally connect with the Holy Spirit and to use playing cards in order to get a "yes" or "no" answer to a question. It's best to master a simple form of divination before going on to a more complex one. If you are interested in becoming an astrologer, the divination practice described in Lesson 23, which comes after this one, will help to prepare you. In fact, this practice is a good prerequisite to any other form of divination training.

Divination is an intensive telepathic communication with the Spirit of Truth. This is why telepathy training between two people should precede divination training. Never attempt divination in any form until you have mastered a basic level of human to human telepathic communication. The reception of information from a source outside of yourself feels different than the type of internal mental dialogue which can take place within your own imagination. When you do get to the point of training yourself in divination practice you want to have the experience of knowing that you are receiving messages from a source other than your own subconscious mind.

Cards may be used both in divination and in basic training for telepathy. And for these practices you only need standard playing cards. This is a deck made up of suits of red hearts, red diamonds, black spades, and black clubs. Don't use "Zener cards". They were supposedly designed for psychic training, but they're ineffective. The Zener deck consists of cards each of which presents one of five black symbols, all on a white background. These symbols are a star, a circle, a square, a cross, and symbol made up of three wavy lines. These five symbols look too similar to lend themselves to distinct visualization. Zener cards superficially look mystical in a pseudo-scientific way. But really they are a poorly conceived tool for psychic training. They only create confusion.

In telepathy you are projecting and receiving *thought-forms*. A *thought-form* is an idea or mental impression that can be perceived by your mental consciousness. These thought-forms must be vivid and distinct from one another. The value of standard playing cards is that half the deck is black and half the deck is red; and this can be use to inspire two distinct visualizations. Think of the binary language of computers: it consists of ones and zeros. Well, you are going to learn the binary language of telepathy using red cards and black cards. The red cards represent fire and the black cards represent ice. These suggest two vividly different visualizations, and thus two different thought-form pictures which can't be confused with one another. The psychic Christian think-tank members who developed this system of psychic development started to train themselves in telepathy by using Zener cards, but they eventually threw away the Zener cards and started using standard playing cards, the kind you can find almost anywhere.

When you practice telepathy or divination do so in an environment that is safe and free from distractors. The ideal environment would be a windowless soundproof room in which the walls, furniture and floor are all middle gray in color. However, that might not be realistic for you. So do what you can to remove distractors. Remove anything that is a bright color which does not need to be there. Put your cell phones and other electronic devices in another room. Don't have drinks which are hot or cold in the room. Only allow some room-temperature water for drinks. Try to find a space that is free from pets and persons who might demand attention. Draw the curtains. Keep the lighting as dim as possible while still allowing you to see adequately.

Training Practice: Basic Telepathy Training

This training exercise is complex and difficult. It also requires a study partner. Yet if you can make it through this exercise successfully, it will be a major breakthrough in your psychic development.

Expect to spend at least three full days doing this.

Day 1 is spent studying the description below of the exercise.

Day 2 is spent doing the preparations for the exercise.

Day 3 is spent doing the exercise itself. You should know that most teams of study partners spend more than three days on all of this. It takes as long as it takes.

If you and your study partner aren't really committed to developing psychic abilities, you might want to stop at this point. To break through the psychic threshold requires a strong feeling of commitment and a resolute intention to succeed. However if you are determined to go forward, I would suggest that you approach this as a game. This training practice can be fun to do. But it is a game with rules and structure that must be learned before you play it.

To reiterate a point made earlier, telepathy training should precede divination training. Before you attempt divination you should establish a degree of telepathic connection with another person. In divination you're receiving mind-to-mind communication from the Holy Spirit of God. In telepathy you're receiving mind-to-mind communication from another person. When you reach a point where you begin to sense that you are actually mentally connecting with another person through telepathy, this is an important breakthrough. In order to go on to divination you don't have to be highly skillful with telepathy, but you do need to achieve the breakthrough where you experience communication which has come from a mind other than your own. You must have the reality of this experience.

This telepathic communication is actually taking place between the superconscious minds of two persons. It is person to person. Once you have this experience, you can routinely open your mind to the Holy Spirit. When you have become fully receptive to the Holy Spirit, you can then easily attune your mind to the mind of Jesus Christ, who is the ultimate authority over this world.

You might consider the possibility that the second coming of Jesus Christ is not the physical return of his body to the world, but rather it is the manifestation of His psychic presence in the world, which is perceived by those Christians who have trained themselves to communicate telepathically with Him.

The Spirit of Truth arises from the Holy Spirit, and the Holy Spirit comes from God. One problem in some types of divination is that you don't necessarily know whether or not the information is coming from the Spirit of Truth or merely your own subconscious mind. God is not an imaginary friend such as what a child would have. As a psychic Christian, you desire to commune, not with an imaginary friend, but with actual God. The subconscious mind is powerful but also childlike. Like a child it may play tricks, pretending to be a source of divine knowledge. This can cause confusion. But if you start off with telepathy training, you come to know when the information is coming from a source outside of yourself. This may be something you have to experience in order to fully understand it.

Find a standard deck of playing cards and make sure it has an even number of red and black cards. Invoke your awareness of God through prayer and meditation. Ask God to consecrate the deck of playing cards to make it receptive only to good influences. Then visualize the deck of cards bathed in glowing white light.

There needs to be two people to do basic telepathy training. Before you and your study partner start this training, the two of you need to do three preparations. These are:

- An empathy drill
- A visualization training drill
- A dry run to master the protocols.

First Preparation:
The empathy drill

You and your study partner make a long list of everything you have in common. Don't put down anything on this list which you don't have in common. For example, let's say that you don't like spinach but your study partner does, then don't put spinach on the list; but let's say that you both like carrots, so carrots do go on the list. Make this list ridiculously long. Spend several hours putting it together. At first ask mundane questions like, "What are your favorite foods?" Some topics that can be covered are favorite books, favorite songs, favorite historical figures, favorite celebrities, favorite sports, and so forth. Have a long conversation and find out all the things you have in common. They don't have to be big things, they can be small things.

Eventually get around to talking about the bigger issues of spirituality and philosophy. But in this conversation, only focus on the things you have in common. Don't argue about what you don't have in common. Telepathy arises naturally from empathic connections, so firmly establish empathy between yourself and your study partner.

Second Preparation:
The Visualization Training Drill

This has to do with learning the visualizations for the red cards and the black cards. To do this preparation you'll need a bowl of ice cubes, a candle, a piece of black paper at least as large as a playing card, and a similarly sized piece of red paper. You'll also need a deck of standard playing cards. With these items you'll be able to teach yourself the binary language of telepathy.

Life on Earth is binary in the sense that we have a continuing cycle of day and night, day and night. The day is bright and warm, the night is dark and cold. But we need them both. The two visualizations that you'll learn in this preparation are designed to mimic this natural dualism. One fact that you should know is that the intuitive right hemisphere of the brain is hardwired to the left hand, and the logical left hemisphere of the brain is hardwired to the right hand. The significance of this fact may make sense to you as you move forward in this training.

First start with the black card visualization. You will base this visualization on your memory of an experience you will create. The experience is black/cold/ice. Get an ice cube and hold it in your right hand as you stare at a black piece of paper, associating this image of blackness with the cold feeling in your right palm.

Next work on the red card visualization. The experience you create for this is red/warm/fire. For this you use the candle's warmth, so that (without burning yourself!) you hold the palm of your left hand near the flame to feel the warmth; do this as you stare at a red piece of paper to associate the color red with the warm feeling in your left palm. You have been warned to please be careful!

Go back and forth between the red/warm/fire experience and the black/cold/ice experience. The more you do this the better. Take a deck of playing cards and shuffle them. Then go through the deck one card at a time. When you get a black card you hold the ice in your right palm briefly as you look at a black piece of paper. When you get a red card, hold your left palm briefly near the flame while staring at the red piece of paper. Go through the whole deck this way so that you imprint yourself with black/cold/ice in your right palm and red/warm/fire in your left palm.

Next, put out the candle and set aside the ice cubes so you can concentrate on practicing visualization. Reshuffle the deck and start over. When you draw a black card you'll close your eyes and visualize a black piece of paper. You'll imagine (or remember) the cold feeling of an ice cube in your right palm. When you get a red card, close your eyes and visualize a red piece of paper, imagining (or recalling) the feeling of the flame's warmth in your left palm. Go through much of the deck this way. You should practice this until you can, at will, hold a clear thought-form in your mind which is inspired by either a red card or a black card.

Third Preparation:
A dry run to master the protocols

Now you must learn to memorize the protocols. When you actually start telepathy training you will follow a set of exact protocols. You and your study partner will sit at a small table across from each other so you can see each other face-to-face. In advanced telepathy training you would eventually learn to communicate telepathically without seeing your study partner's face; advanced telepathy partners can communicate to each other from many miles away because distance makes no difference. However, in this beginner's telepathy training, you need to be able to see your partner's face; this is because you are learning to slowly go from sensory-based communication to extra-sensory communication. This is actually a big leap. This can be very emotional. So you need to make this transition one step at a time. That's why you need all these preparations.

The third preparation you need to do is a dry run. Before you get into the actual use of telepathy, you need to do a dry run in which you're only pretending to use telepathy. In this dry run you each will take turns being the Receiver and the Sender. In this preparation, you aren't going to try to actually send or receive, you'll just practice the protocols of telepathy training. When you've become comfortable with the protocols, each taking turns pretending to be the Sender and the Receiver, then you can go on to the actual telepathy training. But do practice this dry run until the protocols become habitual. When you are doing the actual telepathy training you'll want to be able to concentrate upon the thought-forms, not the protocols. So spend as much time on the dry run as you need to, until you have completely familiarized yourself with its routine. The Protocols are listed below, so memorize them completely before doing the dry run.

Telepathy Training

When you go onto the actual telepathy training, make sure of certain things. You must be sober when you do this, and you can't be hung over from drinking too much the night before. Drugs like marijuana stay in the system for days or weeks. So if you're in the habit of using recreational drugs, you'll have to dry out completely or you won't be effective. You must be well rested when you do this, and you must be healthy. If you are stressed out, or have anxiety about some issue, you may not be able to concentrate. So do this when you are healthy, clearheaded and sober.

Before you go into the training session, you and your study partner should pray together and meditate for a short while. Once you are done meditating, stand up close to one another and place the palms of your hands together; that is, the palm of your right hand will be touching the palm of your study partner's left hand, and the palm of your left hand will be touching the palm of your study partner's right hand. (This may feel a little awkward at first, but it will create a subconscious telepathic connection between you.) You and your study partner will do this by holding up your hands at about the level of your shoulders, palms facing forward; then you will both push your hands forward until the palms of your hands are gently touching. While making eye contact, hold the palms of your hands together like this for about thirty seconds. Most people will feel a slight charge of Gaian life force surge between them when they do this. Psychic Christians call this "priming the pump." In the old days, if you used a water well, you had to pour water down the pipes before you could pump water up from an underground aquifer; that was called priming the pump, so this is an analogy. Here you are using the Gaian life force to form an initial psychic connection. At this point you will feel a slight emotional connection with your study partner, and you'll both be ready for the training.

Make sure you have the right attitude. This is not about showing off. Do this training in private. At this time in your training it's best if you don't practice in front of other people. It should just be your study partner and you. It'll be easier to concentrate that way. Try to make the environment you work in as free from distractions as possible. You want to be calm and serene as you do this. Assume the point of view you would have if you were playing a pleasant game. No matter what, don't get angry with one another. Don't invalidate yourself or your study partner. Don't set goals, just experience the results whatever they may be. Some students get positive results right away, for others it takes time. Even if the telepathy training doesn't go well at first, you should enjoy this as a pleasant social experience with your friend. Don't bring any fear or negativity into this. Be relaxed and content as you perform this practice.

Sit in your two chairs with a table between you. Decide who will be the Sender by flipping a coin. Again touch the palms of your hands together, this time the Receiver will place his or her hands, palms-upward, on the table and the Sender will place his or her hands, palms-downward, gently onto the palms of the Receiver. Again make eye contact and hold your palms together for about thirty seconds. The training session will officially begin after the Sender shuffles the deck.

The Protocols

1. After shuffling the deck, the Sender looks at the top card to see whether it's black or red. The Sender holds the card so that the Receiver can't see it at any time. When the Sender sees what color the card is, the Sender closes his or her eyes and appropriately visualizes either red/warm/fire or black/cold/ice. When the Sender has a clear thought-form in mind, the Sender out loud says "ready."

2. The Receiver practices scan/subvocalize/cognize in this way. The Receiver closes his or her eyes and scans the mind of the Sender. *(This scan is similar to when you were practicing remote Palm Healing. Put your hands up with your palms facing forward. Imagine that beams of light go from your hands into the Sender's forehead.)* When the Receiver feels a connection with the Sender's mind, the Receiver opens his or her eyes then subvocalizes the question, "Fire or ice?" The Sender does not answer this question with words spoken out loud but rather continues to answer the question by focusing upon the appropriate visualization with eyes closed. After subvocalizing, the Receiver keeps his or her mind blank and waits a few seconds for a cognition. Typically the cognition is made up of a single clear cognate. But accept the cognition in whatever form it comes. The cognition may come as a

clear mental-image picture, or it may just be an intuitive impulse. Your intuition might express itself through the simple act of guessing. Furthermore, instead of seeing a picture in your mind, or even having an intuitive hunch, what may happen is that you will feel a sensation of warmth in your left hand or cold in your right hand. Remember that the right hand is black/cold/ice and the left hand is red/warm/fire. No matter what way you read the Sender's thought-form, don't spend more than a few seconds making the choice. If you don't receive a clear cognate in your mind, simply make up a guess. Finally out loud the Receiver will say either "fire" or "ice."

3. If the Receiver has cognized or guessed correctly, the Sender says "hit." If not, the Sender says "miss." Then the Sender shows the face of the card to the Receiver. After that the Sender places the card on the table face down. If it's a hit, the Sender places it in a pile at his or her right. If it's a miss, the Sender places it on a pile at the left.

4. After you've gone through the deck, add up the hits and misses. If you're merely guessing, you should average 50/50, that is, 50% hits and 50% misses. If more than 50% of the cards are hits, that's an indication of telepathy. But to know for certain that you are moving in the direction of telepathic skill, you need to practice this over numerous sessions and keep an exact record of your scores.

Comments: Only do one training session per day, never more. If you and your study partner can meet everyday, that's fine, but try to meet at least once a week as a minimum. You both should have at least that level of commitment. If you do these training sessions too often they may become boring and your scores will go down. But if you think of this as a spiritual ritual, and enjoy the spiritual connection created during this practice, it becomes enjoyable in the same way as meditation. Thus you won't become bored.

In the research think-tank that developed this system, they found that some students got positive results doing this very quickly, but others took a much longer time. In some cases study partners had to go through more than a dozen training sessions before they got the results they wanted.

There's a certain psychological barrier that can get in the way of this. You've been told all of your life that your thoughts are your own and nobody else can know them. This privacy of thoughts is in some way desirable. Some people subconsciously fear that if they start to read other people's minds, or allow others to read their minds, then it will be an end to this privacy. But you should realize that you aren't really going to lose the privacy of your thoughts. When you are performing the drill, you are specifically giving the Receiver permission to read only one thought-form in your mind, the one that you are intentionally holding in your awareness. Your thoughts are still your own. But there can be this emotional barrier. Such fears are groundless, but nonetheless, this can be a big deal for some people, and it may take some time to overcome it.

If you don't seem to be making progress after half a dozen training practices or so, there are some things you can do. First, go back to the three preparations for telepathy training described above and do them again in a more intentional way. You can't be sloppy about this. If that doesn't work, then you may have to go back into this handbook and look again at the lessons to see if there are any concepts explained which you didn't fully understand. Look back at the training practices and make sure that you've done them correctly. You have to master all the other training practices before you start doing the telepathy training or you may not get positive results. If you've skipped some of the training practices, or failed to perform them exactly as described, that could be why you're not getting results.

If you work enough at this, you will eventually get to a point where you're having success. The researchers who developed this system worked out a methodology with teams of telepaths where they could communicate exact messages with 100% accuracy, and distance made no difference. But don't worry about achieving a 100% success rate in this type of beginner's telepathy training. If you reach a point where you and your study partner routinely achieve a better than 70% hits with this, you should call that a success.

What you're looking to achieve in this drill is the experience of reading another person's mind with your mind. So your own subjective experience will determine when you choose to end this training practice. Therefore, you and your partner will decide when you've achieved success.

Once you've had this interpersonal telepathic experience, you'll have more confidence and certainty in receiving psychic information from the Spirit of Truth.

. Lesson Twenty-Three .

Years ago when his group first developed this technique, I met up with my friend James and we did the telepathy training technique described in Lesson Twenty-Two. It was an early version of the method, but it worked, and I found the experience to be amazing. I had a small but significant psychic breakthrough. I developed the ability to sense what other people were feeling, even when they were concealing their feelings. For an insensitive guy like me, this was a big deal. I don't always know what other people feel, but when I need to, I can sense this. And this ability has changed my life profoundly.

Comfort Zone

After you've succeeded with telepathy training, you can go onto this training practice. Divination is not for everyone, and if you don't feel 100% comfortable with this training practice, after you've read this lesson go on to the next one.

Divination

In this technique you use standard playing cards to answer questions which can be answered with "yes" or "no". The deck you use does not have to be complete, but you must make sure that it has an even number of red cards and black cards. Each time you attempt a clairvoyant divination, follow this exact psychic scanning procedure of scan/subvocalize/cognize.

1. Evoke your awareness of God.

2. Say a prayer asking God to reveal the Spirit of Truth to you through divination.

3. *Scan* through the deck looking briefly at the face of each card. Then turn the deck over.

4. *Subvocalize* a question which can be answered with "yes" or "no".

5. Shuffle the deck until you intuitively sense (*cognize*) that you should stop.

6. Don't cut the deck, simply deal out seven cards from the top of the deck.

7. Do the reading in this way: a majority of red cards means "yes", a majority of black cards means "no".

Only ask one question per reading. Do no more than one reading a day. Don't ask trick questions or questions to which you already know the answer. Don't use divination to achieve answers which you could have arrived at through other methods such as research or logic.

You may ask any question to which a definitive answer may be given.

Examples

- Will it rain on my home tomorrow?

- Will this number win the lottery?

- Did the dealer lie to me when he told me that the car he showed me has no major problems?

- Will my home team win the game tomorrow?

- Are my lost car keys still in the house?"

However, don't ask questions to which the answer would be too subjective. For example don't ask, "Should I propose marriage to my girlfriend?" Whether or not a marriage proposal is a good idea is too *subjective*. Whether she agrees to the proposal or rejects it, the results might be either good for you or bad. If she agrees, whether or not the marriage turns out be a good one is something for which only you could know the answer, and that answer would only come from experience. Choose questions which can be answered *objectively*.

The more specific the question the better. Instead of asking, "Will it be profitable for me to buy this stock?" instead ask something like, "Will this stock increase in value over the next month?"

Of course this brings up the issue of ethics again. Our contemporary society is obsessed with greed and materialism. Although there's nothing wrong with using your psychic powers to enhance your ability to make a living, you need to take into consideration the ethical issues in doing so. Some traditional Christians feel that it's morally wrong to have wealth.

Personally I think that a misinterpretation of the Bible to believe that love of money is the root of all evil.

Although greed certainly does inspire unethical behaviors, money itself is morally neutral, it is merely a tool. Like any other tool, it can be used correctly or abused.

Although irrational greed certainly is the root cause of many problems in our present world, I'm convinced that Jesus Christ does ultimately intend that most of us live in a state of prosperity and joy. Of course, whether or not you experience prosperity in the world will depend upon your personal walk with Jesus in this lifetime.

So there's nothing wrong with using your powers to achieve prosperity and joy, but you should consider the ethical consequences of how you do this. If you're uncertain about the ethics of doing something, you can always pray for guidance. But you *should* love the good that money can do.

But don't make important life decisions based on divination techniques until you have achieved a reliable level of skill as a psychic. If your divination practice can't reliably answer questions like, "Will my favorite team win the game tomorrow?" then you haven't achieved a high enough level of psychic skill to use divination to make critical choices. First become skillful at repeatedly getting accurate answers to small questions before you start using divination to answer big questions.

The real purpose of divination isn't to get you to give up your free will; its purpose is to better attune your mind to the Holy Spirit. The idea here isn't to get God to make your choices for you. Divination practice provides a formal structure for communication with the Holy Spirit. This structure builds a strong link between your mind and the Holy Spirit.

Many students stop divination practice after they experiment with it for a little while. This is because they come to realize that in their walk with Jesus Christ they can trust their enhanced intuition. So they don't need the mechanism of divination anymore.

Divination is really just a type of physically active prayer

This type of divination technique is really a type of game. Some highly psychic persons find that they don't respond to it. And if it doesn't seem to work for you, don't worry.

Some Psychic Christians become experts at divination and do remarkable things with it. However, on a personal level, divination should not be allowed to become a crutch for you. You may choose to stop using divination after your mental bond with the Holy Spirit is strongly established. Once you feel that you've achieved an appropriate concordance with your own inner divinity, you can better co-create your life with God's help.

. Lesson Twenty-Four .

One of the anonymous psychic Christians responsible for the development of this system of psychic training was a man who I met when he was in his seventies. He told me about his background. He said that he had been a soldier who worked for the US Defense Department in covert operations. He never told me anything about what was involved in those covert operations, but he did say that he had been extensively trained in what they called "trade craft" which involved things like hand to hand combat, weapons training, intelligence gathering techniques, assassination methods, interrogation techniques, concealment, creating false IDs, developing intelligence assets, military tactics and strategy. He said that for emotional health reasons, he was taken off of active duties. But because of his trade craft training, the defense department still wanted to keep an eye on him. So they assigned him to the Defense Department's psychic research program. They reasoned that this would keep him out of trouble but still on the payroll where they could keep tabs on him.

However, the Defense Department didn't fully appreciate how powerful the training in this psychic research program could be. This man and his friends in the program developed their psychic powers, and as they did so, they began to feel a distrust for the government. Their psychic powers revealed to them the extent to which the US government had become corrupt and treasonous. These newly trained psychics became aware that satanic occultists were involved in the government at the highest levels, and that these satanists were enemies of Christianity and the Constitution of the United States.

When the Defense Department ended its psychic research program, this man and his friends went "off the reservation" changing their identities and disappearing from the prying eyes of the intelligence community. Eventually they hooked-up with a group of Christians who were interested in psychic abilities and began to reorganize this Christian group as if it were a non-violent military unit.

What occurred was a fusion of ideas from different systems of psychic training. This Christian group first evolved from a centuries old secret society of heretical Christians who used structured forms of ancient Christian prayer. In modern times, they had been exposed to the ideas of Edgar Cayce and Reiki healing. When these ex-military Remote Viewers joined this group, this group's techniques for psychic development became super-charged.

They began to train themselves to use their psychic awareness to develop new forms of structured Christian prayer and meditation to combat these satanic occultists. This Christian group is now organized like a military black-ops group, but they don't use violence. They use their psychic powers to do psychic warfare with the satanic occultists who have become the psychic bullies who terrorize and degrade our world.

This book is part of a strategic plan made by these psychic Christians to win this spiritual war that is now being fought for the future of our world. This book is an attempt to inspire other good-hearted persons to train themselves to oppose these satanic, occult practicing, psychic bullies.

Psychic Kung Fu for the Followers of Christ

The term *Kung Fu* comes from Chinese root words which translate to mean *a skill achieved through effort*. It's also a name associated with martial arts training. I have known some Christians who are psychic Kung Fu masters. They know how to defend themselves and others by using advanced psychic abilities. What I am going to explain here are some techniques that they have described to me. You will only be able to take advantage of these techniques if you have mastered your own basic psychic powers. To use these techniques safely and effectively you need to have at least studied the previous lessons in this book. The description of this system of Psychic Kung Fu will take place in lessons 24 through 27. This will give you some idea about how psychic self defense can be used in a more expansive way.

Christian Chant for Reinforcing Psychic Power

The purpose of this practice is to spiritually prepare a psychic warrior to do battle with Satan's demonic army. Here you will coordinate physical hand and arm movements with a repetitive Christian chant which is synchronized with specific visualizations. It's done over and over to generate positive spiritual energy.

You can do this with different affirmations. What I'm going to describe here is the chant as it has been done by certain Christian psychics who I know. But other versions of this can be created. The idea always is that you combine chanting with physical gestures and visualization.

This particular chant consists of four statements and each statement has its own hand and arm movements as well as specific visualizations. This is the same verse that was described in an earlier lesson.

The light of Christ directs me. The love of Christ enfolds me. The power of Christ protects me. The presence of Christ upholds me.

The hand and arm gestures associated with each of the four lines of this chant are as follows:

Raise your right hand in the air and extend your index finger upward as you say,

The light of Christ directs me.

Using both hands, touch the tips of your fingers to the center of your chest at the heart level as you say,

The love of Christ enfolds me.

With your right hand, make the sign of the cross over your chest as you say,

The power of Christ protects me.

Raise both arms in the air over your head with palms open as you say,

The presence of Christ upholds me.

Note: Traditionally the sign of the cross is made with your right hand. You touch your forehead, bring your hand down to your belly button, then touch your left shoulder and finally bring your hand over to your right shoulder.

The purpose of this four step practice is to awaken the Holy Spirit within you. There are also four visualizations which go along with this chant. You say this chant with your eyes closed. You can do this sitting or standing, whatever feels most comfortable for you. Most people do this as they sit because it's easier to concentrate on the visualizations that way. By saying this chant you spiritually affirm your loyalty to Christ. *The more loyalty that you feel for Christ the greater shall be your access to his miraculous powers.* So to some extent those powers become your own. Know that in performing this practice you are transmitting psychic information to Christ and to the body of Christ which is all of Christendom. This is a way of energetically communicating to Christ the intensity of your loyalty to Him and His cause.

The visualizations go like this

When you hold your right hand up with the index finger extended, you visualize that the tip of that finger glows with a white light that shines out in all directions, symbolizing that Christ is the light of this world.

When you touch the center of your chest with your fingertips, you imagine that Christ is hugging you with his arms around you.

When you make the sign of the cross, you imagine that it

turns into a shield in front of you.

When you hold your arms above your head, you imagine that Christ is in front of you ascending heavenwards along with you.

Do this chant in a slow deliberate way over and over again until you feel the energy level in you rise. You may do this with your study partner if you have one. This is most effective when it is done by a group of people sitting together in a circle. When done as a group there is a group leader who speaks a line of the verse out loud and then the others immediately respond after hearing him or her. There is a pause after each line of the verse is spoken so that the visualizations can be concentrated upon. The leader will also determine how long the chanting should go on. Typically this can be done for as much as ten to fifteen minutes. But you should do this only for as long as it feels comfortable. It should be done in a state of reverence for Christ. After you are done, open your eyes and concentrate on breathing normally for a while.

. LESSON TWENTY-FIVE .

Some wealthy and aristocratic satanists are possessed by demons known as Arch-Demons. A person possessed by such a demon is often the head of a coven of wealthy satanists. Such covens are really more like financial groups or micro-corporations. When the possessed person dies, the Arch-Demon possesses another coven member, who then becomes the new coven leader. So the human coven leaders come and go, but the same demon stays in control of the coven.

I once heard a story about the death of a powerful coven leader who was possessed by such a demon. While on his death bed, as he was about to die, the coven leaders gathered around him. Channelling through the man, the demon spoke, and said the name of the man that he would next possess. The demon then went out of the dying man and entered into his next victim, who then began to channel the words of the demon. The newly possessed leader then lead the other important coven members out of the bedroom to have a conference elsewhere in the mansion. Some less important coven members stayed behind with the dying man.

At last the dying man spoke saying, "I can't believe it, I'm finally free. Oh, thank God it's gone from me."

Then the dying man, finally freed from the demon, said a

prayer. He renounced Satan and all of his demon followers. He professed his belief in Jesus Christ. He asked Christ to forgive him for all of the many terrible sins that he had committed as coven leader. He asked to be saved by Jesus. Then, with a peaceful expression on his face, the man died.

The coven members who witnessed this were shocked by the former coven leader's death bed conversion to Christianity. Some them immediately left this satanic coven to convert to Christianity. One of these ex-satanist Christians told me this story.

Pray for the Demon Possessed World Leaders

I think that this story illustrates a point about demons. There are powerful world leaders who do terrible things. They do great harm to humanity and to our world. As Christians we are advised by Christ to love our enemies and to pray for them. This is good advice because it's not the human hosts who are doing the evil, it's the demons that possess them. And thus the most powerful action you can perform to put an end to evil leadership in this world is to pray that world leaders be freed from demonic possession.

Some people try to solve the world's problems by trying to come up with better political or economic systems. But this never seems to work because the demon-possessed world leaders always undermine all of these reform movements. I'm not discouraging anyone from trying to make the world a better place. But I do have to point out that you will never be able to encourage political or economic reforms until you deal with the matrix of fear that controls the demon-possessed world leaders.

Some Christians believe that the Second Coming of Jesus Christ will be His physical return to the world, coming down from the sky. That would be wonderful, to be able to stand in His presence and acknowledge His glory. But I also consider the possibility that the Second Coming is a metaphor for a renaissance of Christian spirituality. One in which Christians transcend religious dogma and develop a more intensive spirituality, perhaps through psychic training.

So the training practice for this lesson is to pray to Jesus Christ that He free the demon-possessed world leaders from the Arch-Demons that control them. Word this prayer in whatever way seems right to you.

Perhaps something like this:

> *Lord Jesus Christ, thank you for the many blessings that you have given us. Thank you for your protection. We ask now, that according to your will, please free the demon-possessed leaders of our world from the influence of Satan. We seek no harm to any human being. May the demon possessed be freed and unharmed. But according to your will, Lord, may the demons themselves be destroyed. May their demonic forms and demonic influence be erased from this world. May all of the people of our world be freed. And may all glory go to you our Lord, truly.*

Remote Exorcism

You should read the rest of this lesson, but if you don't feel

100% comfortable with the idea of exorcism, you should not experiment with this. The practice described in this part of the lesson is not essential to the subsequent lessons. You may wish to feel more confident in your psychic skills before you try this.

This practice differs from traditional exorcism in several ways. Unlike traditional exorcism, you don't need to be a priest, and you don't have to be physically present when you exorcize a demon from a demon-possessed person. You can exorcize the demon that possesses or overshadows a person while you are in a remote location at any distance from that person.

And the demon-possessed person need not know. Furthermore, in this case, you don't need permission from the individual to exorcize a demon which is possessing him or her. This is because demons have no authority from God to possess any human being. However you do need permission from Christ to exorcize a demon.

And the power of God is present everywhere. So you can remotely exorcise a demon without the demon-possessed person even being in your immediate environment. There is no ethical requirement that you inform that person that you are performing an exorcism. This is because demons are psychic parasites so that anyone is better off without being demon-possessed. And although some persons actually desire to be demon-possessed, this goes against the will of God and thus they are morally obligated to let go of their demons.

However, before attempting a remote exorcism, you should

pray to Jesus and ask for His guidance and strength in doing this. And the remote exorcism is really just a form of structured prayer. It is Christ who has the authority to remove demons. What you are doing here is asking Christ to free a possessed person from a demon. And because of the serious nature of this, you are making this prayer in a formal and methodical way.

In the case of some Christian Churches, what they call demonic exorcism may be merely a self-created psychodrama. Some Christian ministers are very negative and judgmental in their preaching. Such ministers, in the name of God, verbally condemn people that they think of as sinful. They talk of God's wraith coming down on them like fire and brimstone. A fire-and-brimstone preacher who goes on and on about the existence of demons is in effect making a hypnotic suggestion to a congregation member that he or she might be demon-possessed. Someone with low self esteem might respond to a fire-and-brimstone sermon as if it were a hypnotic suggestion. So then that congregation member acts out as if he or she is demon-possessed. This is followed by the preacher commanding this self-created demon to leave. And this too is like a hypnotic suggestion. But no real demons are involved.

However, there are real demons, and they do sometimes possess persons. Another name for this is *overshadowing*. And there are techniques for dealing with these real demons. You don't need to chant verses in Latin, throw Holy Water on the person or wave a cross in his or her face. This nonsense is for the horror movies like *The Exorcist*. In real life, to exorcize a demon all you need is faith in Christ, some scripture quotes and some knowledge of psychic ability.

It's interesting to note that the root words for exorcism originally didn't mean to cast out a demon. Originally the word exorcism meant to call forth a demon. Occultists call forth demons to command them to do their bidding. But slowly the demons take over the lives of occultists who command them. Then it is the demon who is in charge. This is one of many ways in which a person becomes demon-possessed. In every case of demonic possession, the individual has at some point consented to be demon-possessed. Usually individuals don't fully comprehend the consequences of their occult experiments. And drug addicted persons may become susceptible to demonic possession without consciously comprehending what has happened. But you can free a foolish person who has allowed himself to become demon possessed.

At this time in our world, many, if not most of the powerful world leaders are suffering from demonic possession. This is true of politicians, corporate CEOs and religious leaders of all faiths. Celebrities and News Personalities often suffer from demonic possession. Many powerful world leaders join secret societies as a way of gaining wealthy and power. Once they are in these secret societies, they are subjected to occult practices in which they become ritualistically overshadowed by a demon. After that takes place, it is the demon who is making all of the important decisions for that person. Our present day world is literally being run by demons. This is why our planet has become much like a living hell.

There are some covert groups of good-hearted psychic Christians who do battle with these demons. This work is actually very dangerous and difficult. You would not want to try to take on any of these Arch-Demons unless you are highly skilled. It's best to take on lower ranking demons who possess ordinary persons before you attempt to take on the Arch-Demons. But the future liberation of this planet will come about by the elimination of these powerful demons from our world leaders.

It is very important that you never use your psychic powers to attack another human being. You must never intend harm for the human being who has become demon-possessed.

The process of exorcism works like this. You make sure that you have reinforced your psychic shield. You use prayer and scripture to separate the demon from its host. You then kill the astral body of the demon so that the consciousness of that demon is forced back into its own world or dimension.

In the Bible there are many quotes about Jesus doing spiritual battle with demons. Consider this one below from Luke 4:33-36:

33 And in the synagogue there was a man, which had a spirit of an unclean devil, and cried out with a loud voice,

34 Saying, Let [us] alone; what have we to do with thee, [thou] Jesus of Nazareth? art thou come to destroy us? I know thee who thou art; the Holy One of God.

35 And Jesus rebuked him, saying, Hold thy peace, and come out of him. And when the devil had thrown him in the midst, he came out of him, and hurt him not.

36 And they were all amazed, and spake among themselves,

saying, What a word [is] this! for with authority and power he commandeth the unclean spirits, and they come out."

Memorize quotes such as this if you are to attempt this type of psychic exorcism.

The process goes like this

1. Reinforce your psychic shield through visualization and prayer.

2. Pray to Christ asking for permission from him to perform exorcism for someone you believe to be possessed.

3. Make a light psychic contact with the possessed person by holding a piece of paper in your hand that has the person's name written on it.

4. Use your psychic insight to sense, see or visualize the demon which is overshadowing the possessed person. Sometimes you can actually see a shadowy form leave the possessed person. Or you may sense the presence of the demon without having any visual perception of it. Another method is to have a grey screen in the room and with eyes open look to see if any visual impressions appear on the grey screen.

5. In the name of Jesus Christ command the demon to leave.

6. When you see or sense the demon clearly, repeat the Bible quote over and over until you see or sense that the demon has been cast out. These demonic astral bodies are horrifying to behold. You will have to repeat the quote at

least twice because the demons always resist. Repeat the verse as much as necessary. And you can use multiple verses. The verse above isn't the only one.

7. Close your eyes and visualize yourself killing the astral body of the demon with a sword, spear, axe or bow & arrow. For some reason, it's best to only use weapons which existed at the time of the historical Christ. Of course, you bring these psychic weapons into being with your imagination, they exist only in your imagination, but they are real in some sense because they are extensions of your psychic power. You may support your visualizations with subvocalization. When you strike the demon, actually make hand and arm gestures as if you were really in combat. But you don't have to hold an actual sword or such in your hand, just hold an imaginary weapon in your hand and make the appropriate arm gestures. In your mind's eye, see the astral body of the demon burst into flames and disappear.

8. Afterwards, send healing energy to the exorcised person so that he or she remains calm.

9. You then return to normal consciousness and write down exactly what you experienced.

10. After that you take a shower or bath. At the very least wash your face, hands and feet. Follow this ritual cleansing with prayer in which you praise Christ and express thanks to Christ. Give all the glory to Christ and none to yourself.

This is actually best done with four experienced Christians

psychics. The first psychic makes a light psychic contact with the possessed person. And when the demon comes out of the possessed person, this first psychic uses psychic powers to keep that person calm. The second psychic repeats the Bible quote over and over again until the demon leaves the possessed person, and its best to keep on saying the quote until the demon's astral body is destroyed. That way the demon won't be able to repossess the person. The third psychic kills the astral body of the demon. The fourth psychic is a guard who kills the astral bodies of any other demons who might come to the aid of the demon who is being exorcized.

Exorcism is dangerous for persons who lack experience in using their psychic abilities or who are weak in their faith. This is not a joke. Don't try this unless you are fully trained and prepared. Demons are real and do have power. And poorly skilled exorcists do sometimes come to harm. Consider yourself warned.

Here is another useful Bible quote. But when using this quote, instead of visualizing that you kill the demon's astral body with a sword or such, imagine that the demons go into swine which then run into a body of water and drown. As you visualize the pigs running into the water, wiggle your fingers and move your arms as if to mimic the running of the pigs. You have to be very confident with your psychic visualization skills to do this.

1 And they came over unto the other side of the sea, into the country of the Gadarenes.

2 And when he was come out of the ship, immediately there

met him out of the tombs a man with an unclean spirit,

3 Who had [his] dwelling among the tombs; and no man could bind him, no, not with chains:

4 Because that he had been often bound with fetters and chains, and the chains had been plucked asunder by him, and the fetters broken in pieces: neither could any [man] tame him.

5 And always, night and day, he was in the mountains, and in the tombs, crying, and cutting himself with stones.

6 But when he saw Jesus afar off, he ran and worshipped him,

7 And cried with a loud voice, and said, What have I to do with thee, Jesus, [thou] Son of the most high God? I adjure thee by God, that thou torment me not.

8 For he said unto him, Come out of the man, [thou] unclean spirit.

9 And he asked him, What [is] thy name? And he answered, saying, My name [is] Legion: for we are many.

10 And he besought him much that he would not send them away out of the country.

11 Now there was there nigh unto the mountains a great herd of swine feeding.

12 And all the devils besought him, saying, Send us into the swine, that we may enter into them.

13 And forthwith Jesus gave them leave. And the unclean spirits went out, and entered into the swine: and the herd ran violently down a steep place into the sea, (they were about two thousand;) and were choked in the sea.

14 And they that fed the swine fled, and told [it] in the city, and in the country. And they went out to see what it was that was done.

15 And they come to Jesus, and see him that was possessed with the devil, and had the legion, sitting, and clothed, and in his right mind: and they were afraid.

16 And they that saw [it] told them how it befell to him that was possessed with the devil, and [also] concerning the swine.

17 And they began to pray him to depart out of their coasts.

18 And when he was come into the ship, he that had been possessed with the devil prayed him that he might be with him.

19 Howbeit Jesus suffered him not, but saith unto him, Go home to thy friends, and tell them how great things the Lord hath done for thee, and hath had compassion on thee.

20 And he departed, and began to publish in Decapolis how great things Jesus had done for him: and all [men] did marvel.

Mark 5:1-20

. Lesson Twenty-Six .

The Full Armor of God

10 Finally, my brethren, be strong in the Lord, and in the power of his might.

11 Put on the whole armor of God, that ye may be able to stand against the wiles of the devil.

12 For we wrestle not against flesh and blood, but against principalities, against powers, against the rulers of the darkness of this world, against spiritual wickedness in high places.

13 Wherefore take unto you the whole armor of God, that ye may be able to withstand in the evil day, and having done all, to stand.

14 Stand therefore, having your loins girt about with truth, and having on the breastplate of righteousness;

15 And your feet shod with the preparation of the gospel of peace;

16 Above all, taking the shield of faith, wherewith ye shall be able to quench all the fiery darts of the wicked.

17 And take the helmet of salvation, and the sword of the

Spirit, which is the word of God:

18 Praying always with all prayer and supplication in the Spirit, and watching thereunto with all perseverance and supplication for all saints.

Ephesians 6:10-18

Training Practice

Take the Bible quote above and use it as the basis for a visualization where you physically act out putting on the armor. First say the quote out loud. Then close your eyes and imagine that you are putting on the armor. Physically act out as if you were doing so. Imagine that you put on the breastplate. Shod your feet. Take up the shield. Pretend that you are putting a helmet on your head. Do this whenever you wish to reinforce your psychic shielding.

. Lesson Twenty-Seven .

Freeing Persons from Satanic Remote Influencing

Again, you should read this lesson, but if you're not 100% comfortable in doing this practice, don't do it.

For this practice you will need a pair of scissors or clippers. They don't need to be sharp, but they must work.

Presently, satanic occultists use their psychic powers to manipulate political leaders, corporate CEOs, celebrities and other important social leaders. This practice of manipulation is called remote influencing. The practice of remote influencing is complex but the psychic practice for freeing persons from remote influence is fairly simple. So it's hard to manipulate people psychically, but simple to free them.

You will be combining physical actions with visualizations that you create with your imagination. Close your eyes when visualizing. You may support your visualizations by subvocalizing what you wish to visualize.

First, pray to Jesus Christ asking that the person in question be freed from satanic control. Ask for Christ's protection and the protection of His angels. Then visualize. The visualization for this works like this. Close your eyes and imagine that you see the person who you believe is being psychically manipulated. Make a light psychic touch with that person, do this by (physically) raising your right hand and reaching out as if you were actually touching him or her. Imagine the source of that manipulation. You can picture the manipulator as a cartoonish devil, a man in a black cape with a hood, a reptilian alien or anything else you want to. Remember that you are speaking to your childlike subconscious mind. Imagine that the manipulator is like a puppet master who has strings that lead down to the person he's manipulating. With your imagination, picture that you are cutting the strings. As you imagine this, physically snap the scissors or clippers open and shut. By this I mean that you are to combine imagination with actual physical actions. The manipulator will try to re-tie the strings. So visualize this. After he does this, cut the strings again. And again as you visualize this, physically snap the clippers. Then take in a deep breath and blow out strongly. As you do this, imagine that the manipulator is blown far away off into space until he disappears. Visualize the liberated person walking around happy and free. Give all credit to Jesus Christ and say a prayer of thanks.

. LESSON TWENTY-EIGHT .

Read or reread the four *Gospels* of the *New Testament*. If you want to you can listen to an audio recording. Continue on to Lesson Twenty-Nine only after you've done this.

If you have a study partner, you may periodically discuss what you've been reading. Obviously it will take you a few days, or longer, to do this. Do this even if you've studied the Gospels before. You may use other reference materials to help you with your understanding of the Gospels. But study them again even if familiar with them. With your psychic awakening that has taken place, you might understand them anew.

I do know that some Christian psychics believe that everything in the Christian Bible can be explained by *ETs*, that is, *extraterrestrial intelligence*. This would mean that advanced extraterrestrials have been guiding humanity through the Old Testament Hebrew religion and then through the New Testament Christian religion. The snake in the Garden of Eden story would represent hostile reptilian aliens. Advanced extraterrestrial powers would explain all of the miracles described in the Bible. But I'm not suggesting that you have to interpret the Bible in this way.

Years ago, when I was doing a radio program on the air, I

did several shows on extraterrestrials. I did one radio show with a psychologist about why people have difficulty with accepting this possibility. There is a tremendous amount of information suggesting the possibility that extraterrestrial intelligence is in some way influencing human affairs. But, of course, you don't have to believe in ETs in order to be a Christian or to be psychic.

Personally I don't feel any need to have an intellectual understanding of Christ in order to pray to Him. The Christian ET theories do make it possible to explain the miracles of Christ in a literal way, but I prefer to try to understand the meaning behind the miracles. For example, the story of Jesus walking on the water is poetically metaphorical and has inspired many people to do what seems impossible.

You don't have to interpret the Gospels in a literal way if you don't wish to. It might make more sense if you can consider that the Gospels are a combination of myth and history; or you can think of it as a true story. Jesus often used parables and analogies in His teachings. For persons who are very literally minded, this may feel confusing. You need to realize that you don't need to have a full intellectual understanding of the Gospels. This rereading of the Gospels is about connecting with a *feeling* of spiritual love.

The Gospels are a love story. They are the story of God's love for His children. Reading the Gospels is a way to feel God's love for you. You can intellectually reject or accept whatever you read there. This is not about religious indoctrination. This practice of reading the Gospels is concerned only with helping you *feel* a loving spiritual presence.

The purpose of the Gospels is to awaken you to your relationship with the living God. Concentrate on the loving nature of this story. Be aware of the spiritual presence that is with you as you read the Gospels. The Gospels are not really about the past, they are about the present time. They are inspirational stories designed to make you more aware of your present-time relationship with the Holy Spirit. They are a doorway that allows God to enter into your life. They are a way to psychically attune yourself with the Holy Spirit.

Do this reading of the Gospels as quickly or as slowly as you like. When you feel that you are done with this, go on to the next lesson.

. Lesson Twenty-Nine .

In the Gospels there are quotes from the Bible consisting of statements made by Jesus Christ. In some Bibles they put the words of Jesus in red. When alone or with a study partner, relax yourself and read the words of Jesus quietly out loud. This will attune your mind psychically to His divine mind. Do this systematically until you've gone through all of the quotes of Jesus in the four Gospels. Don't worry about whether or not you understand the meaning of the quotes. *It is the physical action of saying them out loud that matters because this is a psychic attunement.*

It may take you several days to do this. Don't think that you have to do this all at once. Once you've completed this, go on to Lesson Thirty.

Note:

Only Jesus Christ can teach you the advanced techniques for psychic development. And He teaches every one of His students in a unique and different way. But you need to have a means to receive communication from Him in order to receive these advanced teachings. And Lesson Thirty teaches a technique for this. But completing Lesson Twenty-nine is a prerequisite to this final upcoming lesson.

. Lesson Thirty .

Seeking advice from the Christ

Ultimately, as a follower of Jesus Christ, you want to periodically seek the guidance of Christ, especially when you are facing important activities in your life. This is especially true if you are engaging in psychic warfare or are involved in covert political actions. It's also true if you intend to have great wealth and worldly power.

If you've actually made it this far in the course, you probably have the ability to become a powerful person if you choose to, but that is between you and Christ. With power comes responsibility, and Christ's guidance can help with that. So you are wise to seek guidance directly from Christ.

Go to a quiet place free from distractors. Place one hand on the Bible. Hold a pen in your other hand. Have a notebook in front of you. Close your eyes and say a prayer for guidance from Christ. Word this any way you choose. Open your eyes and practice stream-of-consciousness automatic writing. When you are done, read what you have written, drawn or scribbled. Look for messages there.

This is the final lesson in this book, because from now on, *Christ Himself is your teacher*.

APPENDIX

Christian Talking Table

Before ending this book, I thought that I would tell a story that might convey something of the culture of the secluded groups of psychic Christians. Growing up I was exposed to a number of groups who practiced psychic abilities. Some of them were satanic occultists. They wanted to train me to be one of them. With the help of some psychic Christians, I escaped that fate. Through the help of my Christian friend James, I was introduced to several groups of psychic Christians. In this experience I became aware of a secluded and unique culture.

I'm going to describe something that I've seen used by a couple of different groups of Christian psychics. One group was very old, going back hundreds of years. And they claimed that this practice went back at least to the 1700s. But back then the official Church would have considered it to be a heretical practice. However, I think that at least some modern Christians would find this practice to be of interest. The idea is that you use the Talking Table as a means to receive guidance and information from the Holy Spirit.

A traditional Talking Table would be built by a skilled

carpenter who is a faithful Christian. The carpenter would prepare himself with prayer and meditation before constructing the table. This may sound similar to a ouija board but the tradition of Talking Tables in heretical Christianity is much older, by centuries. The Talking Table is built through a sacred process involving prayers so that demons and ghosts won't go near it, also so that only the Holy Spirit can act through it. So it's not a ouija board.

It is constructed thusly:
The tabletop is circular and is about twenty four inches wide. It has four legs and each leg is about forty inches high. The four legs are also attached to each other with multiple cross braces which make the table steady. Four Christian symbols are carved or written at equal distances from one another at the very edge of the tabletop. On the northern edge there is a Christian Cross. On the southern edge there is a Chi Rho symbol. On the eastern edge there is the Ichthyic Christian symbol of the fish. On the western edge there is the word Christ written in ancient Greek. Close to the edge of the table are two concentric circles which have been drawn or carved. Within these circles are contained letters, words and numbers. They began at the northern edge and move around in a clockwise fashion all the way around to end in a completed circle. These would be: *a,b,c,d,e,f,g,h,i,j,k,l,m, n,o,p,q,r,s,t,u,v,w,x,y,z,no,9,8,7,6,5,4,3,2,1,0,* and *yes*. At the center of the table is a circular area with a surface that has been sanded smooth and polished. Most of the space of the tabletop is taken up with this polished area.

I realize that this might be difficult to visualize so I will reiterate. The polished circular area at the center is surrounded by the two concentric circles which contain the ABCs, the word *no*, the numbers nine through zero and the word *yes*. Outside of the concentric circles are the four Christian symbols at the four edges of the table top which indicate the four directions of north, south, east and west. And I should note that the four legs of the table also coincide with these four directions.

Traditionally after the table had been completed, a group of Christian psychics would meet and say prayers to consecrate the table to the service of the Holy Spirit.

If you were to consider using this practice you should know that the table is best located in a private room where there are no distractors. It would be good if it were located in a room where prayer and meditation is regularly practiced.

The table requires a pointer. The pointer is made thusly. Take a large and finely made martini style glass. Ritualistically wash and dry the glass. Around the edge carefully wind a thin strand of copper wire so that the wire is firmly attached. Have the end of the wire pointing strait outward from the glass for about three inches. Once the pointer has been constructed, it should be consecrated with prayer to the service of the Holy Spirit.

The Talking Table is operated thusly. Because you are consulting directly with the Holy Spirit, appropriate prayers should be said prior to the consultation. The glass is placed upside down on the table. It should be able to slide easily across the polished surface. There must be three people to operate the Talking Table. There is a questioner and two psychic Christians. Traditionally these two were always one male and one female. The pointer is placed at the center of the table with the wire pointing north. The two psychic Christians stand at the east and west facing each other across the table. The woman at the east and the man at the west. Each holds a Bible in the right hand and places the middle three fingers of the left hand on the base of the glass. They stare downward at their fingers. The questioner asks a question and the two physically respond to the question by physically moving around the table in a back and forth way. And typically they also move their arms and wrists as well. They do this quickly and without analysis or conversation because this should be an act of pure intuition. Through their movement the pointer is also moved. They are being moved by the Holy Spirit, and they feel this in their bodies. This is sort of like a dance as they intuitively move together. And the questioner notes where the copper wire points to as they do this.

So the questioner might ask, "Does Christ give our group permission to remotely exorcise the demon that is overshadowing Jane Smith?"

And the two would intuitively move around until the pointer points at the word yes.

There is an art to asking the right questions. You should never ask questions to which you know the answer. You should never ask questions which are trivial. You should never ask questions that require long answers. It's good to use questions that can be answered with a yes or a no. You can ask questions where the answer would be a number. You can ask questions that could be answered in perhaps two or three words. You can ask questions that could be answered by the pointer pointing in a specific direction. And it is the questioner who asks these question out loud and writes down the answer that is sent by the Holy Spirit through the Talking Table.

I've also seen less elaborate Talking Tables. The ABCs, the word no, the numbers nine through zero and the word yes can be written on a long strip of paper. This is placed on a table with a polished surface. The pointer is prepared as described above. The two psychic Christians sit on chairs near each other on one side of the table. When asked a question, they intuitively respond by moving the pointer around to indicate the answer. In such a case, Bibles should be present and prayers should be used prior to the consultation. This way the Holy Spirit will be evoked instead of a demon or a poltergeist. For this practice to be safe and effective, any persons using a Talking Table should be well grounded in their relationship with the Holy Spirit and highly trained at psychic skills.

I observed a Talking Table being used a number of times for a number of reasons, but there is one story that I recall most clearly. This happened in the early 1970s when I was still a teenager. I knew of a group of Christians who were friends and relatives of the members of a secret society of heretical Christians who called themselves the *Gentle Followers of Mary*. The Christians described below were not actually members of the Gentle Followers, but knew of them. I tell the story of this secret society of the Gentle Followers in my book *Angelic Defenders*. But without going into all the details of that story, this particular group of people, described below, were traditional Christians who had been exposed to a knowledge of psychic abilities mostly through family relationships. They had integrated their psychic practices into their prayer meetings. They knew how to use psychic abilities but were not obsessed with them. Their main focus was on traditional Christian prayer.

A member of this group of Christian psychics had come home one day to find that her house had been broken into. A valuable antique silver cross had been stolen from her personal altar in the living room. And so the group met together to consult the Holy Spirit in finding out who had stolen this cross. I happened to be visiting them that day with my friend James which is why I was a witness to this. There was no anger in any of them toward the thief who had stole the cross. In fact they conducted the consultation almost as if it were a type of spiritual party. Everyone wore masks except for James and myself. But that was a common practice when they met with someone like me who had not been initiated into their particular prayer circle. Anyway, I think they liked wearing the masks.

The two leaders of this group were an elderly man and woman who had been married together all of their adult lives. They were childhood sweethearts who had been in a romantic relationship with each other for as long as they could easily remember. We met in the living room and some music was played as the two of them danced together for a while. They smiled with affection as they gazed into one another's eyes. Everyone in the room shared in the glow of their deep affection for one another.

After that we all left the house to go into an out building that was behind the house. This was a kind of simple chapel of sorts. It was large enough for a small group of people to comfortably meet. I remember that it had no electrical outlets. There were lanterns which hung on the walls which could be lit at night. Also there was a wood stove. But neither was lit that day because the weather was fair and the building was filled with sunlight. It had a Talking Table in it along with some folding chairs. This Talking Table was a particularly beautiful one. It was an antique, red mahogany table with the letters and numbers beautifully carved into it. We all gathered together and spoke some prayers. James stood at the northern edge of the table with a notebook in his hand. Then the man and woman stood on either side of the table. They held their Bibles and placed their hands upon the pointer. The rest of us stood in a circle around them. We each held our hands in a prayer position at the level of our hearts. I could tangibly feel the presence of the Holy Spirit among us.

Then James asked, "If it is according to the will of God would the Holy Spirit now please indicate the name of the thief whose identity we seek."

Immediately the pointer seemed to move around as if under its own power. The man and woman instantly moved the pointer around the table in smooth gestures. James wrote down the letters as they were quickly pointed to. The letters spelt out a man's name. Nobody in the group knew of this man except for the woman whose cross had been stolen. It turned out to be her plumber.

She decided to confront this man herself. Later I would hear the story of what happened. It turned out that the plumber's wife was sick and needed an operation which the plumber could not afford. He had noticed the cross in the woman's house one day while working there, and later came back. He had stolen the cross out of desperation. But he knew of no place he where he could sell it, so he still possessed it. The woman offered to lend him the money for his wife's operation in exchange for the cross, and he agreed. Eventually the plumber did pay off the loan with interest. And all of this was according to the guidance of the Holy Spirit.

I did not tell this story because I want you to create a talking table and use it. In fact, unless you are very deep in your faith and highly trained in your psychic powers, it would be a bad idea to experiment with the Talking Table technique.

What I hope to convey is something of the culture of psychic Christians. There was a time in this world when all human beings were fully awakened to their psychic powers. Our ancestors lived in what could be described as a *Garden of Eden*, an environment of beauty and innocence. But then the snake of temptation tricked some of the people into abusing their psychic gifts and using them through occult practices. The human race fell from grace. Thousands of years went by in which humanity was plagued by wars, slavery and wickedness of all kinds. Then the Anointed Savior came to return humanity back to grace. Now we live in a time where those who have accepted the grace of the Divine Source are free to use our gifts of the spirit in ethical ways. Instead of psychic Christians living in isolated and secluded groups, the time has come when there may be the emergence of many groups of psychic Christians, until this culture becomes the norm, and all of humanity again eats those spiritual fruits which come from the beautiful *Tree of Life*.

For more copies of this book refer to

www.psychicThreshold.com

For more information about the author refer to

www.KerthBarker.com